How To Be Right

The Indispensable Guide To
Making Lefty Liberals History

Thanks to all my style-/taste-/tone-/funniness-/fact-/general-right-wing-soundness advisors without whose help this book would be considerably more rubbish than it is. I'd love to be able to give you their names but they have begged me not to for fear of the 3a.m. knock at the door.

Thanks to evil agent Straus.

Thanks to the cracking team at Headline, most of whom are almost certainly a bunch of ghastly lefties because pretty much everyone in publishing is but who nonetheless have done an absolutely first-rate job on this book and who were, I think, very brave to take it on in the first place.

And finally thanks to my dear, wonderful *Guardian*-reading editor Andrea Henry who is so totally the wrong person to be publishing a book called *How To Be Right*, but who has been absolutely magnificent, a joy to work with and a fund of wise advice (most of which I ignored, obviously) and I just want her to know that, even though she probably thinks I'm an evil, racist, sexist bastard, I think she's great.

How To Be Right

The Indispensable Guide To Making Lefty Liberals History

James Delingpole

headline
review

First published in 2007
by HEADLINE REVIEW

An imprint of Headline Publishing Group

1

Cataloguing in Publication Data is available from the British Library

Paperback 978 0 7553 1590 1

Typeset in Abadi by Avon DataSet Ltd,
Bidford on Avon, Warwickshire

Printed and bound in Great Britain by
Mackays of Chatham plc, Chatham, Kent

Designed by Ben Cracknell Studios

Headline's policy is to use papers that are natural, renewable and
recyclable products and made from wood grown in sustainable forests.
The logging and manufacturing processes are expected to conform
to the environmental regulations of the country of origin.

HEADLINE PUBLISHING GROUP
A division of Hachette Livre UK Ltd
338 Euston Road
London NW1 3BH

www.reviewbooks.co.uk
www.hodderheadline.com

'Neither conservatives nor humorists believe man is good. But left-wingers do.' P. J. O'Rourke

For the Fawn who has to put up with this sort of nonsense ALL the time.

A

Aaronovitch, David (see Why?)

Access (n.)

Isn't it tragic that people from council estates hardly ever go to the opera? Isn't it a crying scandal that museum – and gallery – attendance remains so stubbornly white and middle class? Isn't it a national disaster that only a tiny percentage of the population regularly visits the theatre?

No. It's bloody brilliant. It means we live in a country where we're still free to make our own cultural choices – 'A 12-hour abbreviated version of Wagner's *Ring Cycle* viewed from one of the ten-quid extra-cheap seats; the V&A's new blockbuster exhibition of the eighteenth-century needlecraft, or a wild, pill-enhanced night in the mosh pit watching Kasabian? Hmm. Which one will it be?' – rather than having them rammed down our throats by the State.

But not for much longer. To the leftist ideologues who dictate Britain's cultural policy it doesn't much matter whether our museums and galleries can go on maintaining decent, intelligently-curated collections, whether our orchestras remain world class or our operas can still rival those at La Scala or the Met: elitism (*qv*), after all, is so old hat. What does matter very much to them, though, is enforcing something called Access.

Access is the trendy buzzword you find cropping up again and again in policy documents from the Department of Culture, Media and Sport and the Heritage Lottery Fund. Access is the idol all publicly-funded institutions must worship nowadays because if they don't, they won't get any government money. Access is the doctrine which maintains that right now there are hundreds of thousands of minority groups just dying to get their fix of *Don Giovanni*/Turner/early Sumerian cylinder seals but quite unable to do so because of one of the numerous 'barriers to entry' a heartless, uncaring society has placed in their way.

These 'barriers to entry', so the theory goes, might include: lack of braille/disabled access/signage for the deaf; literate labelling which, of course, cruelly discriminates against people who can't read or don't know any history; a general aura of Victorian civic grandeur and suffocating white-middle-classness which some might find alienating. What Access policy claims to do – at immense public expense, naturally – is to rectify these terrible injustices.

This is why museums these days are forever staging shows on things like West Indian carnival costumes, hospital treatment in the Crimean war (with special reference to Mary Seacole (*qv*)) or graffiti art. And why, when you go to your local art gallery, the latest exhibition is a community outreach project curated in collaboration with Asian textile workers or the mentally ill homeless. And why your nearest stately home has decided to put on a hip-hop, paintballing and Pokemon weekend in a desperate bid to replace the blue rinses with that all-important youth demograhpic.

Access is about blackmailing cultural institutions into dumbing down, wasting money and doing things they're no good at and were never designed for in order to drive away their most loyal, enthusiastic customers and replace them with new audiences who are neither interested nor care. Bullying, manipulative, authoritarian, vindictive, socially-divisive, wrong-headed, costly, philistine, destructive and dumb, Access is the quintessence of left-liberal thinking in general, and New Labour policy in particular. Access is just the sort of phenomenon that explains why this book had to be written.

Access (vb.)

Incredibly annoying synonym for 'get' used by idiots (bureaucrats; government employees; 'Uni' (*qv*) media studies (*qv*) lecturers) who want to make themselves sound more zappy and zeitgeisty and techno-literate.

Americans, Self-Hating

'Gee, please don't hate us. We didn't vote for the guy. We're as embarrassed by our lame duck president and our terrible foreign policy as the rest of you.' If I had a dollar for every American I'd heard coming up with this self-hating, self-exculpatory guff, I'd be richer than Bill Gates. What I want to say to these panty-waists – what indeed I do say to these panty-waists is: 'Get a grip, panty-waists. Like it or not you are the world's only hyper power. With power comes certain responsibilities. And since fundamentalist Islam has declared war on you and all the things you stand for, it is not an option for you to sit on the sidelines buried in your Noam Chomsky or Michael Moore (*qv*) and pretend it's not happening. Claiming moral equivalence between the crimes of George W. Bush and the tyrannical regimes he's trying to overthrow may strike the right note in *New York Times* columns and Ivy League common rooms, but doesn't address the problem. Islamism hates America. It wants to destroy you. Mouthing fine-sounding liberal pieties is not going to make your enemies like you more. It just makes them despise your decadence.'

Angelou, Maya

The world's greatest ever writer – as confirmed by her ubiquity in all GCSE English coursework.

Annoying International Name Changes (see also Beijing; Myanmar)

So some tinpot military dictatorship/vicious communist regime/African toilet wants to change its country's or capital city's name to something more 'authentic'. So what if they do? Let them call themselves 'Fnnnnnzzzz' or 'Melanie' or 'Draculasfangoland' or whatever damn thing they like. But for God's sake don't let's pander to their egos by cravenly following suit. Peking was a perfectly decent name with a nice oriental ring about it. Burma is miles better than Myanmar (*qv*). And, while we're about it, let's bring back Gold Coast, Ivory Coast, Bechuanaland and Tanganyika: so much more evocative, so much more *King Solomon's Mines*.

Anti-Racism (see also Diwali; Recycling; Environment, The; Litter; Mary Seacole)

Principal topic at all state primary schools.

Appropriate (see Inappropriate)

ASH

'Firing smokers is an appropriate and very effective way to stop burdening the great majority of employees who wisely chose not to smoke,' says the American branch of professional killjoys Action on Smoking and Health (ASH).

And so it is, providing you use the word 'appropriate' in its fairly unusual sense of 'grotesquely, almost comically over-the-top, unjust, vindictive, mean-spirited, bullying, puritanical and prissily authoritarian'.

Awareness, Diversity (see also Diversity; Multiculturalism)

If private sector taxpayers had any idea how much of their hard-earned cash is blown by the Labour government on 'diversity awareness' schemes Britain would have a revolution on its hands. The only reason the revolution hasn't happened yet is that no one who works outside the state sector reads the *Guardian*'s Society pages, which are where all the 'diversity' (*qv*) related jobs are advertised.

People who work in government or the public services, on the other hand, are all too aware of diversity awareness. But even if they were inclined to complain about it, it wouldn't do them any good, for their career survival now fully depends on their mouthing the correct diversity-aware pieties.

Diversity awareness is being enforced with a thoroughness which would not have looked out of place in Stalin's Soviet Union and its objectives are similarly inspired by Marxist social engineering. Because society's economic structures are inherently biased in favour of white, able-bodied males, the theory runs, the state has a duty to correct this imbalance through a mix of coercion (quota systems, etc.) and compulsory political re-education.

To this end, the Home Office in 1999 set itself the target that, by 2009, 25 per cent of its workers would come from ethnic minorities. Never mind that the department is a complete shambles, quite incapable of fulfilling any of its statutory duties regarding crime or immigration: the important thing is that its ethnically varied employees are as diversity aware as any worker could ever hope to be, thanks to a series of diversity weeks, diversity awareness courses, a positive action programme to develop staff from under-represented groups and diversity training for 15,000 staff in the Immigration and Nationality Directorate.

Similar rules apply in the health service (see Ethnic Monitoring) and also the prison service. Our prisons may be desperately short of cash and space to imprison all the people who need to be imprisoned. But if you're a prisoner and you in any way qualify as a minority, then by gosh your diversity needs are going to be royally catered for. One typical London prison has on its staff a diversity manager; an equal opportunities officer; a foreign nationals coordinator; a disability liaison officer; and an administration support officer to coordinate the diversity team's efforts.

Apart from the sheer amount of money wasted in enforcing these programmes, diversity awareness has inevitably led to a decline in the quality of service. Workers employed on the basis of race, sex or disability are clearly going to be less effective than those recruited purely on the basis of talent and suitability.

This is precisely what has happened at the Home Office and goes some way towards explaining its breathtaking incompetence. Thanks to its positive discrimination programme, ethnic minorities now make up more than 38 per cent of its head office. Yet their performance in Civil Service exams has been consistently lower than that of white staff. Fortunately, the Home Office has found a way of tackling this woeful discrepancy head-on, in a way which will be wearily familiar to students of liberal-left social engineering practice: it has decided to make its exams easier.

B

Baby Seals

They have big soulful eyes, and darling white fur which makes them look so fluffy and scrummy and pure and innocent against the fresh white snow. But since when was that an argument for not culling* them? Surely if fluffy, white cuteness were a valid criterion, we shouldn't eat lambs. Unless, perhaps, there is some special let-off clause (see also Foie Gras; Lobsters, boiling alive) whereby there are some animals whose deliciousness automatically overrides any moral objections to killing them. You may say that baby seals don't offer this justification. But how do you know: have you ever tried one? Perhaps you should. Perhaps we all should. I'll bet the eyes are a particular delicacy.

*Which the Canadians don't do just for fun, let's be clear here: in Quebec and Newfoundland, Harp Seals are overpopulous, they play havoc with scarce fish stocks and their fur and meat provides a livelihood for many locals.

Bailey, Bill

Charming, talented, funny, likeable comedian. Until, that is, you hear him bang on about foxhunting and George W. Bush and you realise: 'Oh, God. He's just another tedious leftie like all the rest of them . . .'

BBC2's Old Dancing Wheelchairs Ident

You remember the one: three men in red perform athletic pirouettes in their wheelchairs and leave you in no doubt that, paralysed though they may be, they live a much fuller and more athletic life than you do, thus challenging your prejudices about what it means to be disabled. Yes, OK, we get the worthy message. But is it really something we have to have rammed down our throats every time we're sitting innocently at home waiting for a TV programme to start? TV's for vegging out to − not for political-correctness enlightenment.

Beijing (see also Myanmar)

'I'll have a Beijing duck with extra pancakes please.' 'He's a perky little fellow. Is he a Beijinese?' 'I want you to close your eyes and count to ten. And NO beijing.' No: Peking was definitely better. (See also Annoying International Name Changes.)

Belgians, The

Nice, solid people on the whole. Great beer. Invented Tintin. But they really must get out of this unfortunate habit they have of kidnapping young girls, imprisoning them in underground chambers and torturing them slowly to death.

Bendy Bus

Loveable euphemism devised by the authorities in London to describe the unwieldy, spontaneously combustible, standing-room-only, cyclist-crushing, cost-ineffective, time-wasting, traffic-slowing, impossible-to-hop-off-when-you-want-to, revenue-losing, massively unpopular public transport disaster introduced by Mayor Ken Livingstone (*qv*) as a replacement for the capital's much loved Routemaster (*qv*), allegedly in the name of disability rights (*qv*).

Betts, Leah

Leah Betts is the schoolgirl who died from drinking too much water after taking an ecstasy tablet. Awful – but in what way does this extremely rare accident justify poor Leah's parents being consulted every time someone tries to have a sensible discussion on drugs policy reform?

Every year, dozens more children are killed by peanuts, and hundreds more by cars than die as a result of doing E. If you asked their parents, you might well find that some of them were so upset they'd be happy to have packets of KPs banned or motor vehicles forbidden from driving at speeds above 10mph. But the point about living in a representative parliamentary democracy is that we try to base our laws on the interests of society at large rather than the special pleading of distraught individuals.

The vast majority of people who've taken E have suffered no more damage than a bit of jaw-ache, a Wednesday blues hangover and a permanent addiction to mindless repetitive beats. To add to these harmless funseekers' misery by having them tossed into jail, there to spend the next few years of their lives being gang raped in the showers, fed on gristle and powdered glass, and administering oral relief to the Prison Daddy, does seem a trifle excessive.

Bias, BBC

On any given subject you know exactly what the BBC's line will be. If it's covering the Middle East it will be bigging up the gallant

Hezbollah freedom fighters and the plucky Palestinians at the expense of the hateful, damned-near-as-bad-as-the-Nazis Israeli oppressors. If it's covering Europe, it will treat every politician who is not in favour of ever-closer-union as a rabid, swivel-eyed, crypto-fascist loon, and every politician who is as a loveable, clear-eyed visionary with a gorgeous mane of beautiful once-blond hair. If it's covering any kind of war in which the US or Britain are involved, it will be of the view that the enemy are the good guys and that we and/or the US deserve to get our arses kicked. If it's covering anything to do with the environment, it will, of course, conclusively demonstrate that the earth is doomed and it's all the fault of greedy Western capitalists.

None of this would matter if the BBC were just some minority interest channel available to cable subscribers only. But it's not. From the salons of Islington to the streets of Mogadishu and Quetta, people around the world still like to believe that if it says so on the BBC then it must be true.

When, therefore, the Pope quotes a fourteenth-century Byzantine emperor saying something unfavourable about Islam and the BBC sees fit to stoke the controversy by courting the views of extreme Islamist groups rather than moderate ones, the Muslim street takes note that Western liberalism is a crumbling, decadent culture which is afraid to stand up for free speech.

And when a grandmother from Bexhill is trying to decide whether or not it's true that Britain is now largely governed by faceless European bureaucrats, she turns to the good, old, reliable, famously unbiased *Today* programme and discovers that, no, this is just a vile calumny put about by barmy Eurosceptics. In fact, the BBC informs her, the European Union (*qv*) is just a beneficent trading body no more threatening than a Women's Institute bring-and-buy sale.

What's worrying about the BBC's institutional leftism is that the people who work there remain so stubbornly unaware of it. It's not that they deliberately set out to be biased but that they have a tragically distorted concept of where the centre ground really lies. Because the only papers they take seriously are the *Guardian* and the *Independent* and because the only people they hang out with share the same values they do (pro-Palestinian, anti-nuclear, pro-Europe, anti-GM, etc.), they naturally assume that this is the way ALL reasonable, educated human beings think, and that anyone who thinks otherwise must be a right-wing extremist.

BBC balance? A concept about as plausible as compassionate Stalinism, Semitophilic Nazism or red-blooded vegetarianism.

Black History Month

Not Mary ruddy Seacole? Again???

Blair, Tony

Future historians are going to compare his minimal achievements with his career longevity and his (once-)spectacular popularity ratings, do a double take and go: 'Bloody hell. What was that all about?'

Blaming The Victim

Among the Mayor of London's numerous public awareness campaigns is a poster of a weeping rape victim with the message: 'The price of taking an unlicensed minicab.' Quite right too. Stupid girls. Serves them jolly well right for catching the first cab that came along as they were shivering outside the club at 3 a.m. in their skimpy gear and dying to get home.

What they should, of course, have done is hung around

waiting for five hours until a 'proper' cab finally came along – with a proper official fare rate about double the one they could have negotiated from an unlicensed minicab. Yes, those girls had it coming to them all right. They were lucky not to have been murdered. And being murdered, frankly, is what they thoroughly deserved for having wantonly and selfishly tried to circumvent the Mayor of LondON's (*qv*) cherished licensing system, so if these slatterns try it again, they'd better watch out.

Blyton, Enid, The Expurgated Version Of

In a bid to render Enid Blyton's fifties adventure stories more appropriate (*qv*) for the modern world, publishers have made what they call 'slight alterations'. Fanny and Dick, from the Faraway Tree stories have been bowdlerised into Frannie and Rick. The boys in the Famous Five and Secret Seven stories are now required to do housework with the girls. 'Queer' has been changed to 'odd'; 'gay' to 'happy'; and fifteen-year-old Andy from *The Adventurous Four* who used to work with his father full-time as a fisherman now spends his days at school and only helps Dad at weekends. Golly, of course – despite his acknowledged popularity among those audiences which white liberals feel ought to be most offended by him: i.e. Asians and Africans – vanished long ago.

Quite right too. It is, of course, perfectly absurd to expect any child in the twenty-first century to make the huge imaginative leap required to understand that children may have acted and spoken differently sixty years ago. Far better to pamper them and spoon-feed them and reduce their PSP-sapped intellectual levels still further by making everything they read as simple and 'relevant' to their needs as possible.

And while we're about it, why don't we set about bringing

all the other children's classics into line? James 'Biggles' Bigglesworth and his sidekick 'Ginger' – but nothing at all wrong with that – Lacey, they're a bit militaristic but perhaps they could be turned from fighter pilots into flying equal opportunity monitors; Oliver Twist – lest he be mistaken for a racist satire on the Romanian child gangs now infesting London – could become the city's youngest and best loved *Big Issue* vendor; the children in *Swallows and Amazons* could be compelled to wear life jackets more often and never go off sailing without close supervision by an adult who has previously been vetted under the Safeguarding Vulnerable Groups act.

Some books, however, may be beyond redemption. *The Railway Children*, for example, with its wanton depiction of potentially lethal rail track trespass and paedophilia and stimulating images of pubescent girls waving their petticoats at complete strangers, will surely have to join Golly, Bulldog Drummond and *Little Black Sambo* on the Index Librorum Prohibitorum.

Bono

Bono is at a U2 concert and he asks the crowd for some quiet. Slowly, to rapt silence from the audience, he begins clapping his hands and says into the microphone: 'Every time I clap my hands a child in Africa dies.' A voice from near the front of the audience pipes up: 'Well, fucking stop it then.'

British Medical Association

Pushy independent trade union which, because of its august-sounding name, most members of the public innocently assume is some sort of dispassionate defender of medical standards in Britain. It's not. It's there mainly to protect the interests of doctors;

closing ranks when they cock up and grabbing them oodles more taxpayers' dosh.

Broad Social Mix (see also Hothousing; Melting Pot)

Excuse routinely used by impoverished middle-class parents to cover up their shame and embarrassment at not being able to afford to educate their children privately. 'Now I know Kenneth Noye Comprehensive doesn't have the best academic record, and Johnny does find his stab-proof vest gets quite itchy in summer, but it has made him so much more streetwise than if he'd gone to Eton. His best friend's father sells crack, don't you know, and another of the mums is a cleaning lady of all things, and he's not remotely snobbish about it, he just takes it in his stride. Birthdays can be a bit tricky of course. We've decided that Johnny's next one will be at Pizza Express rather than chez nous. I mean, some of the children, really. Talk about "count your spoons . . ." '

Brown, Gordon

Dour, tax and spend socialist who, thanks to the sound economy he inherited from the Tories and the one useful thing he has ever done in his political career – *viz.* giving the Bank of England the power to set the national interest rate – has acquired an undeserved reputation for prudence. Scottish. Looks a bit like a slug with eyebrows.

Brown, Yasmin Alibhai (see Why Oh Why Oh Why?)

Brunstrom, Richard

Dismal rozzer – chief constable of North Wales police – whose idea of a fun day off, as boasted about on his frankly terrifying blog, is to go out with his Automatic Number Plate Recognition team and nick as many people as he can for driving slightly too fast or for possessing tiny amounts of cannabis. Best known, however, for his attempts to prosecute Tony Blair for having once uttered the words 'fucking Welsh'.

Good to see, as ever, that Britain's senior policemen are so very much in tune with the concerns of the taxpayers who fund their salaries, generous overtime bonuses and spectacular pension schemes.

Bush, George W.

As Margaret Thatcher was to alternative comedians in the eighties, so 'Dubya' is to stand-ups today. No political insight or humour required: just say the name and your audience are guaranteed to wet themselves with smug, consensual laughter.

C

Cameron, David

Tory leader; nice chap; has, regrettably, no place in a book called *How To Be Right*.

Canadians, The

Once a proud nation of heroes — Vimy Ridge, Dieppe — the Canadians allowed themselves to be transformed in the latter part of the twentieth century into a bunch of milquetoasts whose sole identifiable purpose was to provide fodder for new *South Park* jokes. Now that they've covered themselves in glory in Afghanistan, though, we take it all back. Mighty Canucks, we love you!

Car Crime

There are two sorts: one minor, one major.

MINOR: vandalism; breaking and entering; joyriding; stealing; torching; driving without a licence; driving without insurance.
PENALTY: usually non-existent, especially given that most of the people responsible for these minor offences routinely give false details which the police can't be bothered to follow up. Nor, in the majority of cases, are the police willing to examine CCTV footage

of cars being broken into, claiming, before they have even seen the footage, that it's not clear enough to secure a conviction (i.e. 'we can't be arsed to look').

MAJOR: speeding; driving in bus lanes; parking in the wrong spot; forgetting to pay your Congestion Charge; driving while middle class.
PENALTY: swingeing fines; penalty points; massive double whammy in the form of drastically increased insurance; immediate loss of licence.

Celebrate Diversity (see Jenkins, Woy)

Chair

Something you sit on.

Chairman

If you're a man, you're Mr Chairman. If you're a woman, you're Madam Chairman. This worked for decades. Nobody was bothered by it. Then suddenly, a bunch of girls decided in the seventies that it would be fairer to name the position after an item of furniture (see Chair) instead. Well it certainly makes me respect women a lot more knowing they're taking such important matters in hand.

Chernobyl (see also Nuclear Power)

Stick routinely used by Green fundamentalists to beat the nuclear power industry. And how much easier their task is made when historians as well-respected as Tony Judt can claim in their books,

'Thirty thousand people died as a result of the Chernobyl explosion of 1986.'

In fact, according to 2005's The Chernobyl Forum, the most authoritative investigation, over two years, by eight UN specialised agencies including the International Atomic Energy Agency (IAEA) and the World Health Organisation (WHO – not a body generally known for underplaying health scares), the facts are these:

- Fewer than 50 deaths are directly attributed to radiation from the disaster, most of which were highly exposed rescue workers.
- No profound negative health impacts to the population in surrounding areas.
- No widespread contamination that would continue to pose a substantial health risk, except in a few restricted areas.
- About 4,000 cases of thyroid cancer, with a survival rate approaching 99 per cent.
- No evidence or likelihood of decreased fertility in the affected population, nor of increases in congenital malformations.
- Other than thyroid cancer no increases in cancer rates in the affected regions.

The report said that up to 4,000 people may eventually die as a long-term consequence of the accident, but stressed that this figure was an upper limit – and ultimately uncheckable because statistically it is insignificant when set against the normal background levels of cancer. (For chapter and verse visit www.chernobyllegacy.com.)

Remember, too, that Chernobyl involved a reactor of a completely different type to the ones used in the West, and that it operated under decaying-Communist-regime safety standards far laxer than any in the United States or Europe. But then Chernobyl has never been about the actual facts. It's just a handy buzzword used to close down the argument (*qv*).

Cheshire, Leonard

Leonard Cheshire – later Group Captain Lord Cheshire of Woodhall VC, OM, DSO, DFC – was the most decorated RAF bomber pilot of the Second World War. His near-suicidal courage was legendary. Once, on a raid over Limoges, he made four dummy passes over a factory in order to signal to the French workers that they should escape before they were blown to buggery. He pioneered the Pathfinder technique of flying low over the target and dropping flares to aid more accurate bombing, took a voluntary demotion in order to command 617 Squadron (the Dambusters) and finished the war having flown a record one hundred and one missions. After frittering away the next decade on high living, wondering how the hell he was going to eclipse a career like that, he was inspired – after caring for a dying fellow airman at his home – to set up the Leonard Cheshire Charity. It is now Britain's largest voluntary sector provider of support for the disabled, has an annual income of £135 million and is active in fifty-five countries.

All in all then, not the sort of chap who deserves being remembered in any way whatsoever. Which is why in 2006 the charity's director-general proposed a rebranding exercise to help 'the young generation know who we are and what we do'. Among the suggested new names were: eQual UK; Equability UK and A-BL UK.

Really, you just couldn't make it up, could you?

Child Seats (see also Directives, EU; EU, The)

Hang on. So just after we've gleefully chucked away the car seats which our children no longer need, we're now told we have to spend thirty quid buying another one for any child we have under twelve years old (or 135cm in height), and that if we don't we're liable to a fine of up to £1000?

Great. And who introduced this brilliant new law? The EU (qv). And why did it introduce this new law? Because someone, somewhere, was nobbled by the car-seat-manufacturers' lobby, presumably. And how many lives per annum, according to our government 'might' – note that 'might', it's not even a 'will' – be saved as a result of this ingenious new policy? 1.5. And how much police time will be wasted trying to enforce this new policy?

Closing Down The Argument

If there's one thing the liberal left is absolutely brilliant at, it's closing down the argument. To understand how this process works, try engaging one of your lefty chums in a debate about immigration. It won't be long before you're accused of racism, which is the equivalent of playing the Lamborghini Countach or Hypersoar or Galactus in a game of Top Trumps: it beats absolutely everything.

Similar rules apply on most political topics you can name. Anti-Europe? You are a xenophobe or a Little Englander (qv). Pro-grammar-schools? You're an elitist. Pro-nuclear? Chernobyl (qv). Worried about the growing use of veils? You're Islamophobic. Suspect the eco-lobby may be overstating its case? You're a climate change denier.

In all the above cases, these insults are used as a way of circumventing debate. 'My opponent is so unspeakably vile,' they imply, 'that his views cannot possibly be taken seriously.' You'll notice that this technique is far more often used by the left than it is by the right. That's because, judged purely on their merits, the right's arguments will almost always win.

Coarse Fishermen

Go on, hands up: how many of you stood up for the hunting folk when the animal rights fanatics were trying to ban their sport? Not many of you, I'll bet. 'Hey, they'll never come for us,' you said. 'Not when we're three-and-a-half-million strong and most of us are honest, salt-of-the-earth Labour-voting types. Anyway, fluffy foxes are one thing. But who's ever going to give a toss about glassy-eyed, cold-blooded creatures like dace and roach and chub?'

Well, sorry to disabuse you, all you coarse fishing types, but as you may recently have noticed bunny huggers don't discriminate. They're after the lot of us: huntsmen; shooters; beaglers; hare coursers; fly-fishermen; coarse fishermen. And once they've had those sports banned they'll be after gardeners who use slug pellets and restaurants which have fly-zapping machines in their kitchens, just you wait.

Coldplay

Artful purveyors of polished, coffee-table wank for the chattering classes; would-be saviours of the planet. Unfortunately, their credentials in the latter field took a blow in 2006 when it emerged that a noble scheme to counteract all the eco-damage done – by things like the vapour trails from their continuous rock-star jet travel and the mountainous piles of *X&Y* discarded by listeners who've finally twigged, 'No it doesn't get better with further listens' – had hit the rocks. Of the 10,000 mango trees planted in India to make Coldplay 'carbon neutral', at least 40 per cent died as a result of maladministration or drought.

Community Leaders

(n.) (euphemism PC): rabble rousers, trouble makers and grievance mongers.

Compensation Culture

We could go on about this for hours, of course. Fat soap-dodgers watching cannily-targeted daytime TV ads offering to make them more money than they could ever accumulate in a lifetime's dole scrounging if only they can somehow negotiate their lardy arses off the settee and out into the street or the supermarket, where all they have to do is trip over a loose paving slab or an ill-placed banana, *et voilà!* Two-bit shyster no-win no-fee lawyers putting their brats through public school on the proceeds. Liability insurance rocketing so sky high that playgrounds are closing, school trips are abandoned and the village fête is cancelled because everyone is so scared of being sued. The death of adventure, of fun, of personal responsibility.

Let's concentrate, though, on the Ministry of Defence. You'd think, being as it's to do with war and killing, that it might take a fairly breezily dismissive line on accidents and injuries. But no, it has been sucked into the system willy nilly.

According to an estimate in *Soldier* magazine, the MOD forks out £600 million a year on compensation claims, which in the last ten years have quadrupled. The Bumper Book Of Government Waste has produced several choice examples, including: £81,000 to four soldiers for badly fitting boots; £3,800 to a woman whose superior leapt from behind a pillar and rugby tackled her during a team-building exercise; £51,000 for six service personnel injured falling out of bed. (And even though it's not strictly compensation, let's definitely mention the £2,500 spent so that an aircraftswoman could retrain as a pole dancer.) Crikey, let's hope we never have to fight another major war. The liability actions would wipe us out completely.

Conger Cuddling

Conger cuddling is the delightfully eccentric English sport in which two teams stand on six-inch high wooden blocks and take turns to knock the opposition off with a twenty-five pound conger eel. Or rather it was. The sport – which for thirty years has been practised in Lyme Regis, Dorset to raise funds for the Royal National Lifeboat Institution – was banned in 2006 after complaints by animal rights activists. 'The RNLI is not prepared to be involved in an event that may be seen by some to be a barbaric throwback due to its use of a dead animal,' said a spokesman for the charity.

Surely the real villains of the piece here are not the animal rights activists – they're mad, we know they're mad, so nothing new there – but the RNLI for caving in so pusillanimously to their demands. An organisation brave enough to rescue mariners swamped by thirty-foot waves ought surely to have the courage when threatened with 'exposure' by a couple of nutters with a video camera to say: 'Go on then. See if we care. It's only a dead eel, for Christ's sake.'

Connexions Card

Sinister government scheme to transfer money from honest, hard-working taxpayers into the sweaty, semen-stained hands of rancid teenagers, in order that they could blow it on yet more of the DVDs and mobile phone accessories they had far too many of already. How did you qualify? Why simply by being aged between sixteen and nineteen years and turning up at school.

In a rare fit of government honesty, Beverley Hughes, then junior minister in the Department of Education, admitted of the Connexions scheme: 'There is no evidence that the originally intended impact on increasing post-sixteen participation in further education and training is yet being achieved.' In other words it was a complete and utter waste of money, which is why in June 2006 the scheme was axed. But not before it had cost taxpayers £72 million, £66 million of which went to the government's friends at their favourite crap-scheme administrator, Capita.

CPS

CPS doesn't actually stand for Criminal Protection Society, though given its recent record perhaps it ought to. While the Crown Prosecution Service can be relied on always to prosecute you if you use racist language, show signs of homophobia, or defend yourself against burglars breaking into your home, it appears hugely reluctant to bring cases against genuine criminals. Perhaps its finest hour came in April 2006 when it chose to prosecute a ten-year-old Manchester schoolboy who'd called his classmate 'Paki' and 'Bin Laden'.

Some might argue that it was overstepping the mark here. But I'd suggest that it didn't go far enough. Like all government organisations, the CPS's primary function is not to serve the country but to build its power base and keep itself in business. What better way of doing so than to extend its prosecutory powers so as to embrace the full panoply of playground insults.

Durr Brain? Lard Butt? Blubber Lips? Minger? Ginger? Four Eyes? Spazzmo? Scoper? (*qv*)

You're nicked, son!

Crayfish (see also RSPCA)

In 2006 an RSPCA inspector rescued a poor helpless crayfish from a suburban drain and took it to an internationally recognised crayfish reserve, Ensors Pool, near Nuneaton, Warwickshire. Unfortunately he'd picked the wrong sort of crayfish. The one he had found was the vicious red-clawed American crayfish. The ones in the reserve were endangered, indigenous white-clawed crayfish which, since the 1970s, the aggressive, disease-spreading American crayfish have been busily wiping out. Animal lovers: the very last thing nature needs.

Danish Flags

Danish flags: they keep them everywhere in the Middle East, obviously, because of Denmark's legendary strong colonial ties with the region.

No. Not really. In truth, by no stretch of the imagination is it conceivable that anyone on the Arab street would normally have in his possession a Danish flag, any more than he would a Bolivian, Tibetan or Zambian one. So how come, during the 'spontaneous' demonstrations everywhere from Syria to Saudi Arabia against the publication of those infamous Mohammed cartoons, they managed to trawl up dozens and dozens of the things to burn on camera?

It was all a carefully orchestrated put-up job, clearly. Only someone exceptionally stupid would fail to realise this, especially had he troubled to cast even the most cursory of glances at the story's background. It started in autumn 2005 when a Danish newspaper *Jyllands Posten*, shocked to hear that a publisher was having enormous difficulties finding an illustrator who dared provide a picture of the Prophet Mohammed for one of its children's books, decided to test the limits of free expression by commissioning a series of cartoons on Islam.

The cartoons were published to stunning indifference. So, in order to whip up the frenzy of indignation they felt the cartoons deserved, a group of Danish Islamists toured the Middle East stirring up trouble. Fearing the cartoons weren't quite controversial enough, they helpfully inserted a few inflammatory images of their own. It was these, far more than the actual cartoons, which led in 2006 to the riots, the death threats and the storming of the Danish embassy in Syria.

So far, so bad. But what really turned this chain of events into a disaster was the way, instead of standing up to this brinkmanship and bullying, the West chose to take the Islamists at their word and apologise for the 'offence' caused. Not one British newspaper dared to stand up for free speech by publishing the cartoons. Their weaselly excuses ranged from the fact that the cartoons weren't funny (they weren't but so what? This was now a news story of international significance so surely the public deserved to be able to make up its own mind what the fuss was about) to the disingenuous suggestion (in the *Spectator* of all places) that to republish them would be needlessly provocative.

For unutterable cravenness, however, the British press couldn't come close to matching the response of the then foreign secretary Jack Straw. By publicly apologising to Muslims for any offence the cartoons had caused, he sent a clear signal to Islamists everywhere that the West is no longer prepared to stand up and defend its core values.

Since when, in any case, was a British foreign secretary responsible for anything printed in the Danish press? Since when, for that matter, was he responsible for anything printed in the British press? In the West we have free speech. Politicians don't have control over anything the newspapers say. We are not subject to the constraints that so often apply in the Muslim world. Well, not yet.

Directives, EU

Rarely a week goes by without some new, restrictive – and apparently permanent and binding – EU directive creeping up on us unawares. How is this allowed to happen? The process of this accumulation of new-EU-laws-by-stealth was once anatomised by *The Times*:

'It is at first denied that any radical new plan exists; it is then conceded that it exists but ministers swear blind that it is not even on the political agenda; it is then noted that it might well be on the agenda but is not a serious proposition; it is later conceded that it is a serious proposition but that it will never be implemented; after that it is acknowledged that it will be implemented but in such a diluted form that it will make no difference to the lives of ordinary people; at some point it is finally recognised that it has made such a difference, but it was always known that it would and voters were told so from the outset.'

Disability Rights

'Disability Rights' is another of those heavily loaded, politically correct challenge-phrases ingeniously calculated to brook no opposition.

'What?' it shrieks at anyone who begs even slightly to differ. 'You mean you DON'T think that wheelchair users should be able to travel by public transport or go to the theatre or see a film or have any fun whatsoever? You DON'T want blind people to be able to read the public safety notices that might very well save their lives? You DON'T want the deaf to be able to understand what's going on at the opera? And I suppose you'll be saying next that all disabled people should be put down at birth or experimented on in Dr Mengele-style death camps, because that's what you are basically, isn't it? An evil, bastard Nazi!'

None of us wants to be disabled. Those of us who aren't look at those who are and think: 'Poor bugger. There but for the grace of God go I' and then feel all embarrassed about having stared too hard or possibly not looked lingeringly and caringly and 'I recognise you as a real person' enough, or whatever it is the strident Disability Rights poster campaign tells you you're meant to do when you see a handicapped person these days. It's this awkward blend of pity and fear which has been so brilliantly exploited by the Disability Rights lobby.

What began as an admirable campaign to make the lives of the disabled less unpleasant has mutated into a shrill, bullying, self-righteous movement apparently hell bent on punishing anyone who has the temerity to have all their bodily functions working properly. So, it's deemed perfectly acceptable to deny millions of Londoners the joy of travelling by Routemaster bus (*qv*) on the grounds that a handful of wheelchair users may not find them practical.

In April 2006, an organisation called the Disabled Persons' Transport Advisory Committee was able to have South West Trains banned from using a certain type of carriage – not even as a stopgap measure to reduce overcrowding – because the lettering on their information screens fell 3mm short of the 35mm minimum required by disability regulations.

In Cumbria, a small village school was forced to exhaust five whole years' worth of its new-building-projects budget installing a compulsory disabled toilet, even though none of the children at the school suffered any kind of disability.

Like green taxes and equal opportunities policy, Disability Rights has proved yet another handy way for the liberal-left to advance its statist, anti-capitalist agenda behind a smoke-screen of social worthiness and decency. It discriminates especially against small organisations (shops, businesses, schools, etc.) which, unlike rich corporations, cannot absorb the extra costs and bureaucracy involved so easily. It loves trashing historical buildings, too, with lifts and ramps and obtrusive signs.

And, unfortunately, this mission creep shows no sign of abating. Under the latest interpretations of the Disability Discrimination Act pretty much any form of bodily inconvenience now technically qualifies as a disability – from a bad back to manic depression to alcoholism to common or garden stress. Indeed, 'Disability' is now a term so loose that according to one government survey 11 million people – one quarter of the adult population – can be described as disabled. Which leaves the other three quarters of us to be crippled by disability legislation.

Discrimination (see also Prejudice)

Discrimination used to be the quality an English gentleman spent a lifetime trying to acquire. It meant discernment – the ability to differentiate between the good and the bad, the refined and the slipshod, truth from cant, the genuine from the fake. Today it means 'being unpleasant to women, ethnic minorities, gay people or the disabled'.

Words are constantly evolving – 'naughty' used to mean 'evil' rather than 'mischievous' – and that is as it should be. But as the Conservative MEP and journalist Daniel Hannan once astutely noted in the *Spectator*, there is something very deliberate, unnatural and sinister in the way the English language has been suborned by the cultural left for political ends. In this case, he pointed out: 'A firm that *discriminates* in favour of properly qualified applicants or a university that insists on good A level results cannot wholly escape the sense that it is doing something dirty.'

Diversity

(n.) (archaic): a state of richness, variety and abundance.
(n.) (current usage): an excuse to nurse grievances at taxpayers'
expense.

Diversity is why your children come home from primary school
knowing more about Eid or Diwali (*qv*) than they do about Easter.
It's why your local council is happy to organise numerous festivals
to celebrate any cultural activity so long as it isn't an English one.
It's why if you live in the countryside and you apply for any kind
of state funding for your church hall or your bowling clubhouse or
your cricket pavilion you won't get it, because the people who'll
benefit don't push the correct 'diversity' buttons: i.e. you're all too
white.

'Celebrating diversity' (see Jenkins, Woy) – as our local councils
so often claim to be doing on our behalf – may sound jolly but in
fact it's just a grindingly politically correct (PC) euphemism for
'state-enforced multiculturalism'. Like multiculturalism (*qv*),
diversity has nothing to do with getting us all to mix it up in one
big happy melting pot (*qv*). Quite the opposite. For 'diversity',
read 'division'.

Typical of this is the way schools, museums and local
authorities choose to target history for specific minorities: Muslims
are encouraged to dwell on the injustices of the Crusades, blacks
are encouraged to want compensation for the slave trade, Chinese
people to resent the Opium Wars, people from the Indian
subcontinent to be angry about Amritsar, and anyone from a
foreign country which has ever fallen under British rule to be
appalled by the Empire. The theory behind this is that it enables
alienated minorities to feel connected with their roots. The reality
is that it becomes an exercise in finger-pointing by the minority

grievance industry, lavishly funded at the expense of the decreasingly amused or tolerant taxpayer.

Diwali (see also Anti-Racism; Recycling; Environment, The; Seacole, Mary)

Principal topic at all state primary schools.

Drop The Debt (see also Rock Stars)

A rich, gullible, well-meaning uncle has lent you £100 million and rather than invest it wisely as the naïve old buffer had hoped you've gone and blown it on whores, drugs, fleets of Mercedes and a fabbo palace with two statues of yourself at the entrance, one made of platinum and Bongo horn, one fashioned from pure pashmina.

You have a suspicion that, when he finds out, your uncle's going to be quite cross. And not unreasonably, either, given that your cousin in Asia has used the same amount of money to build a thriving business which is doing so well that before long he's going to pay your uncle's money back, with interest.

But then, something truly amazing happens. A famous rock star has got to hear of your plight and made up his mind that, being now so very badly in debt you qualify as one of society's dispossessed and are therefore in need of much sympathy. After all, think of all the money you owe your uncle in interest alone. How are you ever going to get back into the black with debts like that?

'Clearly,' says the rock star, 'there is only one solution. Your uncle must "drop the debt".' And sure enough, gullible old fool that he is, he does.

Are you:

a) So chastened by guilt and so touched by your uncle's generosity of spirit that you resolve from henceforward to keep your financial house in order; to spend wisely and frugally; to build your business until it rivals even that of your Asian cousin's?

b) Wetting yourself with laughter at your uncle's stupidity; thinking: 'Well if he can afford to lose a hundred mil that easily, he must be good for another hundred million at the very least!'?

Now put yourself in the shoes of an African kleptocrat dictator, whose sole aim is to take his country's economy for as much money as he possibly can before the inevitable coup when he flees in his private jet to Saudi Arabia or France: a or b? Really, it's a no-brainer.

Drug Dealer, Evil, International

When was the last time you felt threatened by an evil, international drug dealer? Me, I'd say probably never, and I expect it's the same with you. So why is it that time after time when you go to see an action movie – *Mission Impossible III*, say – the deadly villain who's supposed to have you quaking in your boots and longing for his bloody demise is invariably a kingpin of the global narcotics trade?

There are two worrisome things about this, the first being its essential dishonesty. If Hollywood villainy was really representative of our deepest fears, the most commonly encountered baddies would be scary Islamic fundamentalists. But a place as painfully liberal as Hollywood doesn't feel comfortable showing Muslims as the bad guys. It worries that this might be construed as racism which, besides being in itself an unforgivable wrong, might not play too well with the all-important ethnic demographic.

What is more bothersome, though, is the sheer tragic waste. How can any recreational drug user – and there are many – possibly derive any pleasure from the supposedly climactic scene where the drugs kingpin and his factories get blown to kingdom come? We can't, obviously. Not when, as keen students of the laws of supply and demand, we realise what a disastrous effect this would have on street price and availability.

International drugs dealers may be an evil, but they are a necessary one. If they weren't there, who else would fund the private armies which protect the coca crops from kill-joy, US Drug-Enforcement-Agency-sponsored search-and-destroy missions? Who would go to all the expense and effort of processing those coca leaves into snortable white powder? Who would dream up the ever more ingenious ways of getting that powder past the noses of our customs officers and on to the street, so that it can go into those dinky little paper wrappers, safely inside our wallets and then up our nostrils?

It's thanks to those much-maligned evil, international drugs dealers that our parties go with a swing, our gums stay numb and our dinners go on past midnight. Baddies? Nonsense. They're the friends we've never met.

Dying Of Ignorance

One of the great urban myths of the eighties – right up there with the tale of the mysterious female hitchhiker with the suspiciously hairy hands who leaves behind an axe in the friend of a friend's car – was the one about how AIDS was going to kill us all: young, old, gay, straight, it just didn't discriminate, so there was nothing for it but to give up sex there and then and wait for the nineties to arrive.

But, like most urban myths, it just wasn't true. 'AIDS – Don't Die of Ignorance', warned all the scary posters put out by the government. Yet ignorance was exactly what the government was promoting, for HIV was not at all an equal opportunities disease. You were far, far more likely to catch it as a result of playing rude bottom games with a gay man then you were, say, from a straightforward shag between a man and a woman. So why didn't the government say so?

Because then, as now, it didn't want to face up to the politically incorrect truth that AIDS is mostly the preserve of specific minorities. In the eighties, it was gay men whose sensitivities were being protected. More recently it is HIV-positive immigrants (mostly from Africa) who have been largely responsible for the massive spike in AIDS cases during the last decade.

For those of us heterosexuals who didn't get nearly as much sex as we might have liked in the eighties thanks to this irresponsible misinformation campaign, this is indeed depressing. But what's far worse is what it says about the entrenchment of PC within our culture. When journalist Anthony Browne reported the truth about recent HIV cases in a front page story in *The Times*, he met with a conspiracy of denial everywhere from the Government to the BBC and the *Observer*. One government medical advisor, phoning Browne secretly from the Department of Health, told him: 'Ministers won't listen because they think it is racist.'

Those infected immigrants have since 1997 gone on to give HIV to nearly a thousand more people. Most of these new victims belong, of course, to the very minorities whose feelings the government was so concerned not to hurt. How grateful they must be feeling for the government's sensitivity.

E

Elgin Marbles

Global antiquities are far too important to be left in the hands of foreigners. Look at what the Taliban did to the 2,000-year-old Buddha statues of Bamiyan: a world heritage site blown to smithereens in one afternoon in a fit of bring-back-the-Dark-Ages Islamic pique. Look at all the priceless Iraqi antiquities that went missing during the looting of Baghdad. And what about the Armenian medieval cemetery in Jugha, Azerbaijan, its ornate headstones completely obliterated last year by the Azers in revenge for the destruction of Muslim sites?

This is why, whenever some new Greek culture minister comes along (every two months, roughly) to demand the return of what in Greece they call 'the Parthenon marbles', we should hear them out courteously, furrow our brow pensively for all of two seconds and then reply: 'No way. Bog off, Melina/Stavros/Zorba.'

Partly it's a simple question of property rights. The marbles were not, as the Greeks would have it, looted by Lord Elgin in 1801. They were purchased fair and square and what's more if he hadn't bought them and shipped them back to England there would hardly be anything of them left by now. We know this because the ones that stayed behind are a pile of rubble.

Mainly, though, it's the sheer principle of the thing. If we repatriate the Elgin marbles, where do we stop? Do we give the Egyptians back the Rosetta Stone and all those delightful mummified cats? Do we hand the Benin bronzes back to the tender cares of Nigeria? You hardly need to be Colonel Blimp to realise that Western museums have better facilities and take care of their artefacts better than any African one could.

So maybe it's time we stopped feeling guilty about all the priceless objects our gallant Empire-builders have liberated over the years and accentuated the positive. In fact maybe what we should be doing, rather than giving them all back, is heading off to rescue a few more chunks of the world's diminishing heritage before it's too late.

We could reinstall Peru's Inca temples in the Derbyshire Peak District, thus ensuring that never again might any visitor be threatened with kidnap by Shining Path guerillas. We could satisfy Mohamed Al Fayed's deepest desire by plonking the great Pyramid of Cheops directly on top of Harrods and burying him, in true pharaonic style, underneath. We could ship those bits of the Parthenon Lord Elgin didn't manage to buy first time round up to Edinburgh. At last, the completion of 'Scotland's Disgrace' (the mini-Parthenon atop Calton Hill), and the unification of the Athens of the south with the Athens of the north: what a splendid cultural event that would be!

Elitism

1. You're being held hostage by terrorists and might have your throat slit at any moment. Would you rather be rescued by a) the SAS, b) the Iraqi police or c) a team of ordinary members of the public, chosen by ballot — it's so much fairer that way because everyone gets a crack of the whip?

2. There's a tumour on your brain that urgently needs removing. Should this delicate task be performed by a) a neurosurgeon with seven years' medical training and a further five years'

practical surgical experience, b) a hairdresser, butcher, fish-monger, sushi chef, boy scout, whatever, just so long as they're comfortable with sharp blades that'll do me fine or c) a pharmacy graduate from De Montfort University?

3. Your precocious child is reading Shakespeare at three, translating Greek to Latin at four, solving Fermat's Last Theorem at five. Where to educate him? a) Why obviously at the best school money can buy – to squander such genius would be a crime, b) a grammar school, ideally, we'll just have to move to Kent or c) he'll do perfectly well at the local comp. Brighter kids always cope; it's the self-esteem of the less able ones which worries me more.

Unless you're completely bonkers you will have answered mostly a)s – thus automatically rendering yourself guilty of the dread 'crime' of elitism. This linguistic development is one which our forebears would have found puzzling. Not so long ago, it would have been thought barmy not to want to live in a society which nurtured fine minds and strove for excellence. How else could there be progress?

It is, after all, the cultural elite which ensures the survival of all that is best in art, music, drama and literature. It's our sporting elite which wins or used to win us Olympic medals, rugby and football world cups, etc. It's our military elite who undertake our most dangerous missions and defend the nation in times of crisis. It's our political elite who (well, in theory) ensure that we are properly governed. It's our intellectual elite who think up the bright ideas which, with luck, will make us brighter still.

In its current usage, however, elitism has mutated into a catch-all term of disapproval, meaning a combination of snobbery, selfishness and unfairness. What's odd is that many of those who use 'elitism' in this pejorative way – Guardianistas, government ministers, BBC reporters, senior educationalists – hold down jobs which they can only possibly have secured through a very competitive selection process. Maybe we should take them at their word, give them all the sack, shout 'Quis' out of the window and then pass their jobs on, in a much fairer and more egalitarian way, to the first person who replies 'Ego'. No, hang on, that would require an understanding of Latin. Which would be way too elitist, wouldn't it?

Environment, The (see also Anti Racism; Recycling; Seacole, Mary; Litter)

Principal topic at all state primary schools.

Environmentalism (see also Kyoto Protocol; Wind Turbines)

Bossy new world religion based on the self-flagellating principle that unless we make things worse for ourselves things cannot possibly get better.

Ethnic Monitoring

You've made it! After three painful months on the waiting list, you've finally landed a hospital appointment to see a specialist about your piles. Before you do, though, there are a few things the receptionist needs to check with you: your home address, your religion, your next of kin – and finally, would you just mind looking at this list and deciding which category most closely applies to you?

You look at the list with mounting dismay. It includes pretty much every ethnic grouping under the sun, from Andorran and Albanian all the way to Xhosa, Yoruba and Zulu. There's even about half-a-dozen for people who you might have thought would be covered by the word British, including white (Welsh), white (Scottish), and white (Traveller) — but no white (English), predictably enough. And what you'd like to do is grumble to the receptionist about the utter ridiculousness and insultingness of all this, but you know there's no point because a) she doesn't care, and b) hospital staff are so chippy these days that she's bound to think it's a case of the verbal harassment which all the signs on the wall tell you 'This hospital does not tolerate' and use it as an excuse to have you thrown out by security. And you wouldn't want to have to wait another three months to have your urgent bottom problem looked at, would you?

So instead, you sit in the waiting area, surrounded by specimens of humanity who make the cantina scene in *Star Wars* look like a Miss World pageant, fuming quietly to yourself. 'Why in God's name do they need this information?' you wonder. 'What business is it of theirs whether I'm Scottish, Mongolian or Venusian? Surely the only thing that ought to matter is whether I'm a British citizen, and therefore entitled to free NHS treatment, or whether I'm not — in which case I can either pay for it or bugger off to wherever it was I came from and sponge off my own government's coffers instead.'

And how much does it cost to run this ethnic monitoring system anyway? Some people are presumably being employed by the NHS to tabulate and process the information. Other people are being employed by the NHS to examine it and use it — though God knows how — to formulate expensive, meaningless new strategies. Others still are being employed to run these people's departments. Yet more to recruit them, deal with their wages and pensions, and sort out their contracts. Add this all up and it must come to quite a bit. Meanwhile, the NHS (*qv*) goes deeper into the red and the waiting lists grow longer. As do those piles.

EU, The

Warning: there is nothing funny about this entry. It's far too depressing for that.

Whatever you know about the European Union, it's worse than you think. One reason for our surprising ignorance on so important an issue is that we find it so ineffably boring that no one, apart from those involved in the furtherance of the Project, can be bothered to read the small print. Mainly, though, it's because secrecy, disinformation and mendacity have been built into the Project from the very start.

The key thing to understand about the EU is that it was always meant to be an all-embracing political union, never just an economic one. But what its inventors – notably, the former cognac salesman Jean Monnet – realised early on was that no rational electorate would allow its country's sovereignty to be abandoned for the sake of some pie-in-the-sky, pan-European ideal. The whole process of ever-deeper integration, they realised, would have to be conducted by stealth. (Or as Project insiders knowingly call it 'engrenage' – which means 'gearing' i.e. ratcheting up little by little.)

For many years Britain resisted this process. But in the bout of self-doubt which followed the Suez Crisis, the government of a declining, post-Imperial Britain looked towards the Continent, saw what it imagined to be the world's new economic powerhouse, and panicked itself into deciding that it must join this mighty trading group at no matter what cost.

And in order to do so it had to lie to its people. From Harold Macmillan's time, Britain's political leaders were perfectly well aware that this was far more than just a trading bloc, that it was intended to be a supranational organisation which would relieve national governments of much of their powers. But to admit as much, they knew, would never wash with a people as proudly independent as the British. So, over the years, European integration has always been sold by successive British governments to their electorates as an economic issue, never as a political one.

Rarely in the field of political duplicity has a British prime minister lied to his country more blatantly than when Edward Heath (*qv*) told television viewers in January 1973: 'There are some in this country who fear that in going into Europe we shall in some way sacrifice independence and sovereignty. These fears I need hardly say, are completely unjustified.'

Since 1970 when Heath elbowed Britain into the Common Market with no democratic mandate (the subject had barely been mentioned in his general election campaign), all the things he promised would not happen have happened. The key political decisions governing almost every aspect of our lives – from how much we're paid to how we police our borders to what is and isn't safe for us to eat to the way we take our measurements to how we dispose of our rubbish – now stem from faceless bureaucrats in Brussels, and not from our democratically elected representatives in Westminster.

Membership of the European Union has changed Britain immeasurably – and unremittingly for the worse. We have been forced to destroy our fishing industry – and then watch, helplessly, as the seas round our shores, once the richest fishing waters in the world, are devastated by Spanish, French, Dutch and Belgian trawlers (see also Fish). We have signed up to crazy directives which have destroyed our abattoir industry, hamstrung our chemical industry and blighted our landscape with wind turbines (*qv*). We are on the verge of losing our right to drink out of pint (see also Feet, Inches, Pounds, Ounces, Gallons, Pints) glasses and even to decide how we defend ourselves. Membership of the EU has cost us more money (in taxes and bureaucracy) and made us less free.

In our hearts we know this. So how is it that Europe continues to grow inexorably against the objections of so many of its constituent peoples? Because this, like the lying about its objectives, was always part of the plan. The labyrinthine complexity of the European apparatus – the Commission, the Parliament, the Council of Ministers, the Court of Justice – was designed simultaneously to sow confusion and avoid accountability; to enable the EU to enlarge itself regardless of how many 'No' votes its constitution was awarded in local referendums.

What's extraordinary in an age of conspiracy theories is that the greatest modern conspiracy of them all – and one that happens to be true, to boot – has been so pointedly ignored by so many for so long. It's significant that the only serious and thorough investigation there has ever been on the subject – *The Great Deception* by Christopher Booker and Richard North – went unreviewed in every national newspaper.

The European Union has been the single greatest political disaster since the Second World War. This is rather a large and terrifying mistake for anyone to admit to having made. Perhaps too large. No wonder we're all so determined to avoid the issue. 'If only we can all ignore it for long enough,' seems to be the thinking, 'maybe it will magically disappear.'

It won't.

I did warn you it wasn't funny.

'Excellence For All'

Tautological Blairite phrase which sums up perfectly the utter vacuousness of the New Labour project. Excellence is, by definition, a state that only a few can achieve. In order for some to excel, others must perform averagely. 'Excellence for all'? Only a real second-rater could have dreamed up an idea like that.

Exxon Valdez

There's nothing the media loves quite so much as a juicy oil tanker disaster: the stricken ship; the spreading slick; the condemnation, blame, hand wringing and feeble excuses; the obligatory topical newspaper cartoon with the caption 'The Price Of Oil?'; the heartwarming, final-item story on news broadcasts of volunteers rescuing baby seals and wiping the feathers of gunge-swamped seabirds.

Bad, obviously. Sad, too. But strip away all the emotion and cant: how bad and sad are these oil disasters really? In *The Skeptical Environmentalist*, Bjørn Lomborg (*qv*), investigates one of the top twenty worst-ever oil disasters – the running aground of the *Exxon Valdez* in Prince William Sound, Alaska, in 1989, where it spilled 266,000 barrels of oil – and comes up with one or two awkward facts that eco-charities and eco-scientists might prefer you not to know.

For example, though the estimated 250,000 seabirds it killed is indeed a terrible thing, this figure is no greater than the number of birds that die on a single day in the US flying into plate-glass windows; nor yet, than the number of birds killed every two days in Britain by domestic cats. The price of the clean-up was more than $2 billion. Money well spent, you might think, until you learn what actually happened. By way of experiment, some of the polluted beaches were left uncleaned while others were professionally cleared and pressure-washed (which had the unintended effect of killing much of the marine life). Life returned to the polluted beaches after just eighteen months, whereas it took three or four years to do so on the cleaned beaches. This was in line with what oil experts had predicted, but never mind, the public had demanded that something – anything – should be done. Or, as the *Scientific American* put it: 'The public wants the animals saved – at $80,000 per otter and $10,000 per eagle – even if the stress of their salvation kills them.'

Failed Consumer

Next time someone mugs you for your mobile phone, for pity's sake don't blame your assailant. Blame yourself. It's all your fault, see, because by the very act of owning such a high-tech telecommunications device you have been promoting 'the rampant egoism of turbo-consumerism'. And that's not good.

Your poor old mugger, meanwhile, is just the hapless victim of a ruthlessly commercial society in which we are judged by what we consume. When he attacks you and nicks your phone (and your iPod, and your trainers, and your wallet) he is not driven by greed, but by an innocent desire not to be excluded; to be normal. He is not a criminal. He is a *failed consumer*.

When this thesis was given air in the *Guardian* comment pages (29 June 2006) some readers might have been forgiven for imagining it to be a wickedly funny spoof satirising the idiocy of liberal-left thinking on crime and the causes of crime. But then, of course, they would have realised: 'This is the *Guardian*. The *Guardian* doesn't do self-parody. Well, not deliberate self-parody.' Then they would have turned to the author's website and gone: 'My God, he's an actual person.' At which point they would have come to a truly, terrifying conclusion: 'Christ on a bike. This is how the left really thinks!'

Fair Trade (see also Kyoto Protocol; Drop The Debt)

Moral litmus test. If you disagree with it, you are a heartless bastard. But the one thing Fair Trade isn't is fair. Take the Fair Trade coffee which gives you a warm glow of right-on satisfaction every time you drink it, even though it's not quite as mellow as the non-Fair-Trade stuff and 15 per cent more expensive: what you're actually doing is featherbedding coffee producers in relatively affluent places like Mexico (where 25 per cent of Fair Trade coffee comes from) at the expense of needier producers in places like Ethiopia (where there's some Fair Trade but not as much and where the coffee is nicer).

Artificially raising the price we pay to favoured coffee suppliers doesn't make things fairer, it just distorts the market. Nor does it solve the fundamental problem which is that too much coffee is being produced, which keeps prices low, which means farmers can't afford to make a decent living out of it. Subsidising those Mexicans isn't helping them. It's removing their incentive to find a better job in a more lucrative field. But, obviously, no do-gooder wants to know any of these awkward truths. Much better to pay the extra, buy the Fair Trade T-shirt, and tell yourself you're a good and lovely person who really, truly cares.

Faith Schools

'Daddy, is it true that all heathens are doomed to burn in hellfire, that we must smite the Jews, the Catholics, the Hindus and the Muslims with our powerful, mighty swords and that Christ is our only salvation?' my five-year-old asked me the other day.

'But of course it is, my darling,' I replied. 'How well they are teaching you at your Church of England primary school.'

Of course, if this were the sort of thing that C of E primary schools did teach they would have been banned by the government like a shot. Different standards apply in Muslim schools, however. There, it would seem, it is perfectly acceptable for children to be taught that their religion is their primary cultural identity, that non-believers belong to an inferior species known as *kuffar*, that Muslims are Muslims first and loyal British citizens very much second.

When left-wing commentators call for a ban on faith schools because they are divisive and intolerant, what they are really talking about is Muslim schools (and, to a lesser extent, Hindu and Sikh ones). But they daren't actually say as much lest they be accused of racism. And in multicultural Britain, as we know, anti-racism trumps everything: including truth, fairness, social cohesion and the not unreasonable desire of Christian parents in a Christian country to secure for their children a marginally less dreadful education than they get in state schools without the C of E or RC connection.

Feet, Inches, Pounds, Ounces, Gallons, Pints
(see also Directives, EU; EU, The)

Did you know that as from 1 January 2010 using these terms in Britain to describe weights and measures will become a criminal offence under EU law? Probably, you didn't. Rather like those straight bananas, it's one of those meddling-EU stories so preposterous that you think it couldn't possibly be true. There must be a catch, some bit of small print that will somehow let us off the hook and enable us to ignore this particular EU ruling, just like the French do with all the rules they disagree with. But no. The new law is enshrined in the EU's Statutory Instruments (55 & 85/2001) and it will come about. This, despite the fact that repeated media polls have shown that around 90 per cent of the population are opposed to compulsory metrification.

So, a couple of centuries after he lost at Waterloo, Napoleon will belatedly have succeeded in two of his most fervent wishes: to subsume British democracy within a statist, pan-European tyranny; to deny every Englishman his inalienable right to enjoy an ounce of rolling tobacco with his pint of bitter down the pub before he heads home to give his French girlfriend something she could never hope to experience from any of her compatriots – a good six inches of prime English sirloin.

Firefighter

Hmm. I think 'Fireman' was the word you were looking for. Unless, of course, she's a chick – and why shouldn't she be? We'll have none of that discriminatory nonsense round here thank you very much – in which case she's a 'Firewoman'. Or 'Firegirl', maybe, if she's a total babe.

Fish

'Everybody wants to save the earth. Nobody wants to help Mom do the dishes.' P. J. O'Rourke

The greatest ecological catastrophe of our lifetime is happening on our doorstep. From the North Sea and the English Channel to the Irish Box, many of the fish stocks which were once ours as of right are now on the verge of total collapse. Thousands of our fishermen have lost their livelihoods while others are subject to swingeing fines for breaching obscure regulations which seem to have absolutely no bearing on fair play, economic viability or conservation practice. Some species – notably cod – may already be too far gone to recover. And all because in 1971 Ted Heath (*qv*) cravenly chose to surrender our fishing rights in capitulation to an illegal EEC demand so as to secure Britain's entry into what was then known as the Common Market, now the European Community.

So why aren't we taking to the streets in protest? Why aren't questions being asked in parliament every session? Why aren't all the eco-charities making it their number one *cause célèbre*? It's not as though there's any shortage of damning evidence: the fleets of, mainly Spanish, 'flag boats' leaving up to 5,000 miles of gill nets hanging unattended in the deep waters off Ireland and Scotland which render 70 per cent of the catch so badly rotted it has to be thrown back into the sea; the bizarre decision (by a Danish fishery official in Brussels) to allow the Danish industrial fishing fleet to plunder a 40,000-square-mile section of the North Sea which had hitherto been closed, supposedly to preserve cod stocks; the insane quota system whereby fishermen are required to destroy large portions of their catch; the EU corruption, horse-trading, incompetence, maladministration, lies, junk science, greed and vandalism.

None of this needed to happen. In Iceland, through careful management, they've reversed the decline in their fish stocks – including cod – to recreate a thriving industry.

We could have done the same here. Maybe we still can. But we won't. Why? Firstly, because, for all the damning evidence to the contrary, we still cling to the naïve hope that on some level the EU must know what it's doing. Second, because thanks to people like Al Gore we know that there are far, far more important channels for our campaigning efforts. Face it: melting ice caps, flooded metropolises and drowning polar bears may not be a real threat but they are so much more dramatic than boring smelly fish.

Fisk, Robert

This week in the Independent*'s occasional series of travel articles by star writers, we sent our Middle East correspondent, Robert Fisk, to visit the sleepy market town of Appleby-in-Westmoreland.*

So it has come to this? A town, a whole town in northern England and not a single brown face from one end to the other. Not a brown face, not a black face, not a yellow face, not even a coffee-coloured face. White. All of them white. White, the drained, pallid, shade of the radioactive fragments of a US Abrams tank's depleted uranium shell in the frail body of a wounded boy I once knew named Hassan who'd only gone to the shops to buy a cake for his mother's birthday.

I walk on, shaking my head, more in sorrow than anger. Where is the warm, welcoming chant of the muezzin from the minaret? Where is the scent of cumin? Where are the freedom fighters with their cheery, masked faces and their oppression-battling rocket-propelled grenades? Where indeed.

'You look a bit lost,' says a voice. 'Can I help you?'

Lost? Is it any wonder I feel lost in a world where big-boned US marines named Bob and Juan drive their bayonets into the eye sockets of new born babies and then use their eyeballs for games of marbles on concrete made from the ground-down bones of thirteen-year-old boys wrongfully arrested on trumped-up charges while their heads were bowed in prayer.

But instead, with a world-weary shake of my knowing head, I say merely: I only say, 'Where is the mosque?'

'Mosque?' he replies. 'We haven't much call for them round here. You see . . .'

And do you know – such is the remarkable power of the

propaganda campaign being waged by Messrs Bush and Blair – I think this fellow actually believes it. I hope that I can credit my readers in the *Independent* with a little more intelligence, by asking three key questions which, with luck, the editor will decide to splash in 40pt typeface as he generally likes to do with my stuff.

FACT: Appleby is famous for its annual horse fair. Might it not well be that one of those horses was once sold to Mr George W. Bush, who would have ridden it while planning his insane, murderous, international-law-breaking assault on the sovereign state of Iraq?

FACT: There are churches throughout northern England cunningly disguised to look as if they have been there for centuries. Is it so unreasonable to speculate that large sums of money – Big Oil money – might have created this realistic effect?

FACT: On 9/11 not a single person from Appleby was in the Twin Towers when the alleged airliners crashed into them. Coincidence? Or had they been tipped off beforehand by MOSSAD or its chums in the CIA?

Next week: Polly Toynbee visits Las Vegas and is appalled to discover that under Bush's America a once-sleepy desert market town has been transformed into a sleazy capitalist hellhole of female exploitation and worker degradation.

Foie Gras (see also Lobsters, boiling alive)

If God really cared that much about animal rights why would he have made foie gras taste so delicious?

Freedom

Formerly: a state of liberty. Now: an entitlement to services admini-stered by the state, as in, 'freedom to use the NHS', 'freedom from discrimination'.

In his appendix to *1984*, George Orwell explained that one of the most effective ways of suppressing heretical thought was to eliminate undesirable words or strip them of their meaning. The example he gave was 'free'. The word continued to exist in Newspeak, but only in the sense of, 'This field is free from weeds' or 'The dog is free from lice', not in the old sense of 'politically free' or 'intellectually free'.

As journalist/MEP Daniel Hannan has observed, this is precisely what has been done to our language by the liberal left. Words such as 'discrimination', 'diversity', 'community', 'profit', 'public', 'elite' and 'competition' are now so tainted by association with a specific political value system that they have all but lost their original meanings. As Orwell wrote in his appendix to *1984*: 'Newspeak was designed not to extend but to *diminish* the range of thought . . .'

French, The

Who built Saddam Hussein's first nuclear reactors? The French. Who prefer to imagine that in June 1944 they liberated themselves without any outside help? The French. Who devise all the EU's most annoying laws which they expect us to obey but which they themselves completely ignore? The French. Who continually sabotage the West's attempt to present a united front against Islamic fundamentalism? The French. Who aren't pulling their weight in Afghanistan? The French. Whose food only tastes good because it's swamped with butter and cream, which we could all do if we wanted, but we don't because it's cheating? The French. Whose farmers run the EU? The French. Who promised to sort out the Lebanon because it's supposedly 'their' patch but are actually doing bugger all because they daren't upset Hezbollah? The French. Whose women are great to look at – fabulous bone structure – and are always immaculately turned out, but turn into neurotic, hyper-demanding nightmares the moment you try going out with them? The French. Who produce the world's ponciest, most wrongheaded, most incomprehensible and most far-up-their-own-bottoms intellectuals? The French. Who lost at Crécy, Agincourt, Poitiers, Blenheim, Ramillies, Oudenarde, Malplaquet, the Battle of the Nile, Trafalgar, Talavera, Waterloo, the Franco-Prussian War, in 1940 and Dien Bien Phu and have consequently decided to opt out of all further fighting, even though by rights we all ought to be in this one together, because they're a bunch of cheese-eating surrender monkeys? THE FRENCH.

Full Driving Licence (see also Disability Rights)

If you're an employer and you put out a job advert asking for someone with a full driving licence you could well be breaking the law. It says so on the Disability Rights Commission (DRC) website. Apparently you'd be discriminating against disabled people who can't drive but could do the job just as well using public transport. Excuse me. Has anyone at the DRC ever actually tried getting around by bus? Do they know how slow it is? How long the waiting time is? How utterly useless buses are on all but the most basic A to B routes? I don't know about discrimination against the disabled, but this idiot rule definitely discriminates against any company which prefers its employees to do a day's work rather than hang around at bus stops. Mind you, by about 2009, the ruling will be an irrelevance anyway. If the speed cameras keep working at their current attrition rate, there will be no one left with a full driving licence.

Funded By . . .

'Funded by the logging industry/the energy industry/Big Tobacco/ Big Business . . .' Whenever you hear someone's writings or opinions tarred with this brush, pay extra attention to what they have to say: it usually means they've got it so right that their Green/Left-Liberal opponents can't think of any other way to counter their arguments than by sneering innuendo.

This is what philosopher Jamie Whyte calls the 'Motive Fallacy' – the idea that if you have some particular interest (financial or otherwise) in holding an opinion this must automatically render it untrue.

Even more dishonestly, it presupposes that any organisation not funded by big business is therefore completely unpartisan when, in fact, quite the opposite is true. In the ten years up to 2006, for example, the US government spent $20 billion on research programmes investigating man's impact on global warming (qv): considerably more than has been invested by the energy industry trying to prove that it's nothing to do with us. Which goes a long way towards explaining why scientists tend, on balance, to be in favour of theories claiming that climate change is man made and it's a serious danger: that's where the money is.

G

Gays, Proselytising

Some of my best friends are gay, and the reason they're some of my best friends is that they don't keep banging on about how gay they are. Face it chaps (and chapesses): you've won the battle. There is no need, any longer, to go and confront an uncaring world with your gayness so as to prove that you, too, are a Real Person With Feelings who deserves the same consideration as the heterosexual majority. We know.

You've won on *Big Brother*. You've got Julian Clary and Graham Norton. You've had *Queer As Folk*. You write the scripts for *Doctor Who*. You've given us one up the bum many, many times. And we like it, it's great. We surrender. OK?

Yet there are always one or two for whom nothing is ever quite enough. Yes, I mean you: the ones who seem to think it's a national outrage that Second-World-War-era lieutenant-colonels still aren't welcoming you for snogging sessions at their Pall Mall clubs. That there aren't sufficient Tory party blue rinses on the floats at Gay Pride rallies. That homosexual foreplay* isn't yet a compulsory part of the national curriculum.

So you're gay. So what? Get over it. Everyone else has.

---

*'What homosexual foreplay?' asks one of my gay friends.

Geography Teachers

In the good old days geography teachers were reassuringly dull figures in brown corduroy jackets with patched elbows who smoked pipes and droned on harmlessly about oxbow lakes and glacial moraines. They wanted to map the world, not change it. They knew that the only people who studied geography at university were the thickoes who couldn't get in to read anything else. But that was fine by them. That's why they became geography teachers themselves.

Today, though, geography has so little to do with geography that really it ought to be renamed Man Is a Murderous, Fascist, Eco-destroying, Capitalist Bastard Studies, because that's what it's all about these days. Then your kids come back from school insisting you use eco-friendly washing up liquid instead of stuff that actually works and suggesting maybe it's about time the whole family went vegetarian in solidarity with impoverished Bangladeshis.

But can they tell you the capital of Outer Mongolia or point to where Paris is on the map? Can they hell.

Germans, The

From 1939 until at least 1943, Germany was the most powerful military nation on earth. They thrashed the Czechs, the Poles, the Hungarians, the Dutch, the Belgians, the French, the Norwegians and the Greeks; they drove the Soviets back to the gates of Moscow, and they damn nearly trounced the US and the combined might of the British Empire and Dominions to boot. Of course, during that time they were complete bastards. But you can't deny that for all its faults the Third Reich did cut a pretty impressive figure on the international stage.

And now look at them. 'Ewww, nein. Ve cannot commit more

zen five soldiers und a pea shooter to Afghanistan – even though ve are members of NATO und ought to be damned grateful for ze privilege – because fighting is dangerous und someone might get hurt. Und our Luftwaffe cannot fly operations at night because zis vould be in breach of health und safety regulations and zis is nichts in ordnung.'

Yes, after a brief post-war stint as Europe's economic miracle, the Germans have managed to break all records for former-great-power crapness: their politics are tyrannised by Nazi-like Greens with plaited armpit hair who've swapped their hippy VW Combis for expensive hybrid cars with *Atomkraft? Nein Danke!* stickers on the back; they've got no architecture to speak of (and serves them right) because it was all trashed in the war; they're incapable of serving you a hamburger within three hours because half the staff come from East Germany where terrible service is a given; their labour laws are so irredeemably socialist that a keeper who had been sacked for eating several of the rarer species in his zoo took his employer to an industrial tribunal and actually had his job reinstated; there are no decent views left anywhere in the country because they've all been ruined by wind turbines (*qv*); their national cuisine consists of nothing but cabbage, mustard and reconstituted pig. And Goethe wasn't as good as Shakespeare – well probably not; we don't know and can't really be arsed to find out because what's the point of learning German when they're all so embarrassed about The War these days that they all speak English anyway.

And the problem is, we all know where this is going to lead, don't we? What do the Germans do when their nation has become weak and pathetic and they're all suffering from such low self-esteem that the closest any of them get to *lebensraum* is rising early and conquering all the best sunbeds?

Exactly.

Global Warming

According to the government's Chief Scientific Advisor, Sir David King, it's an even bigger threat to the world than international terrorism. According to George Monbiot (*qv*), it's right up there with the genocidal killing of six million Jews. According to Dave Cameron, it's so damn serious that unless we put windmills on the sides of our Notting Hill homes right this instant, then by 2050 we'll all be living in Little Venice – and not in a good way!!!

Clearly then, the only sane thing to do is to take drastic remedial action. We should:

1. Build a wind farm on every upland beauty spot (see Goldsmith, Zac) to show once and for all that prettiness and leisure and views and other such fripperies have no place in an age when the World Is Dying.
2. Raise taxes by at least an extra tuppence in every pound so that the islanders on Tuvalu can build a big wall around the edge to stop themselves drowning under the rising sea levels that we, yes we, have personally created.
3. Don ironic Mickey Mouse masks and NBC suits, smash the windows of our local McDonald's, and boycott every G8 summit until the evil capitalist system collapses and we all agree by international consensus to return to the agrarian age.
4. Murder any scientist who disagrees that global warming is the worst disaster ever and chop all his research into tiny bits so that never need anyone again be exposed to such horrid disgustingness.
5. Send all 4x4 owners to be hung, drawn and quartered, before being cooked and fed to starving polar bears (*qv*) stranded on ice floes.

6. Emigrate to the moon for a couple of millennia – and not even live in nice, exciting, Eden-Project-style geodomes; just in dreary, grey craters and subsist on a miserable diet of cosmic microbes, Clangers and moon dust – to punish ourselves for our planet-destroying impudence and to give Mother Earth a chance to recover – if she ever can – after our dreadful depredations.

But what if the global warming alarmists have got it all wrong?

Global temperatures have, after all, been fluctuating quite naturally for centuries, from balmy, vine-abundant medieval Britain, for example, to the period of global cooling between 1940 and the early seventies which prompted many scientists to predict an imminent ice age. And even though the world is definitely getting warmer at the moment, there is still much debate within the scientific community as to how much of this is man made and how much is due primarily to solar activity. There are also studies which suggest that the beneficial consequences of global warming far outweigh its detrimental ones – for example, a study in 2004 found that if Britain's temperature rose by two degrees Celsius over the next fifty years, heat-related human deaths would increase by 2,000 but cold-related deaths would decrease by 20,000.

This isn't the sort of information being broadcast all that often by the lobby expressing concern about global warming which, as Al Gore (qv) does in An Inconvenient Truth, dismisses any arguments which contradict its views as those of mavericks and nutters. But if the climate change doom mongers are really so sure all the evidence is on their side, why are they so keen to stifle any arguments which threaten to prove them wrong?

Goldsmith, Zac

Posho green activist (see also Monbiot, George; Porritt, Jonathon) with better looks, loads more money and a much more exciting Christian name than George Monbiot, which is why poor George has to say much madder things to get himself noticed. When Zac dies, it is rumoured, his billions will be spent fulfilling his lifelong ambition to purchase every British hilltop above 1,000 feet and decorate it with an attractive, energy-saving wind turbine (*qv*).

Gore, Al

Overindulged loser.

Grade Inflation

Disgraceful, that's what it is. An insult to hardworking kids. They spend the whole summer flogging their guts out; they can barely eat or sleep or play their Playstations for the worry it causes them; and when finally their results come through and it turns out they've earned 300 A*s each, what thanks do they get? Why only some Tory fascist miseryguts moaning on about grade inflation and slipping standards. Well let me tell you, I'm having none of it. The reason for this year's unprecedented exam successes is because kids are working harder than ever before and teachers are teaching better than ever before, and it's time, for once, that we acknowledged a great British success story. Our education system is the envy of the world!

This is the speech made without fail every August by whichever unfortunate happens to be education secretary, but it's all bollocks and they know it is. Walk into a shop. Catch a bus. Watch

Love Island. Try to engage a teenager in conversation. Have you ever come across a single piece of evidence to support the contention that our young are the new master race of academic *Übermenschen*?

If so, this will come as news to many university dons, who now have to spend the first year on remedial teaching to bring students up to standards which ten or twenty years ago they would have achieved before they left school. It will also surprise business employers, who now find that it is common for school leavers to turn up with a string of impressive GCSE and A level qualifications – yet still be functionally innumerate and illiterate.

Here are the raw facts: between 1965 and 1980, the A level pass rate remained steady at around 68 per cent; from 1985 onwards the pass rate and the proportion of top grades began their inexorable rise, from 70.5 per cent in 1985, to 84 per cent in 1995, then up to 96.2 per cent in 2005. The government has yet to confirm rumours that as from 2008 it plans to make its marking considerably tougher: in future an A* will only be awarded after the submission of five Frosties or Cocoa-Pops tokens instead of the previous three.

Gradgrind, Mr (see also Language Teaching In Schools)

He was right, though, wasn't he?

Gramsci, Antonio

Italian Marxist best known for his brilliant analysis that in order for the left to win the political battle it must first win the cultural one. It has. Hence this book.

Greenland's Icy Mountains

Greenland is melting and by 2080 all the world's coastal cities, including New York, are going to end up under water, causing Kevin Costner to grow webbed feet and sub-*Mad-Max*-style pirates to roam the seas on jet skis, power-boats and suchlike from their Heath-Robinsonesque bases, until eventually they're all blown up because that's what happens to baddies.

Well the first bit's going to happen, anyway. We know this because Greenpeace (*qv*) tells us so. At a conference held in New Delhi in 2002, Greenpeace launched a flood (ho, ho) of world-is-drowning stories by predicting a massive rise in sea level of five to seven metres (sixteen to twenty-three feet) due to the melting of the Greenland ice sheet – which, of course, would be caused by evil man and his greenhouse gas emissions.

Before we all start building our arks, though, let's have a look at what the latest report by the UN's (global-warming-obsessed) Intergovernmental Panel on Climate Change (IPCC) has to say. From 1990 to 2100, it says, Greenland's projected contribution to sea-level change will be from −0.02 to 0.09 metres.

By the end of this century, in other words, melting Greenland will have caused sea levels to rise by at most 9 cm (3.5 inches), and might possibly even cause sea levels to fall.

But you're never going to read about this in the newspapers, are you? It just wouldn't create the same splash.

Greenpeace

'Vrrrrrmbump Vrrrrrmbump. Splish. Splosh.' Yes, it's those daring campaigners in their rubber inflatables zooming along in the wake of a horrid Japanese whaling ship and being sprayed by water cannon by evil, slanty-eyed, whale-murdering scum. And look, there goes another pair from the gallant Greenpeace action team, scaling a ginormous nuclear-waste tower and unfurling a banner that says, 'No To Nuclear': that'll put those pesky radioactive polluters in their place! And there they go again, closing up a waste pipe belching industrial effluent. Hurrah for the brave lads and lasses of Greenpeace! While the rest of us just sit around moaning, there they are putting their lives on the line and doing the business. Three cheers for Greenpeace, no, make that seven cheers! How ever would we sleep safely in our beds without you?

This is the second scariest thing about Greenpeace: the fact that you're supposed to think that everything they do is wholly altruistic and unmitigatedly for the good. At Glastonbury, you have to watch their propaganda videos on the big screens, and woe betide you if you don't cheer their PR stunts with the requisite righteous enthusiasm. When they campaign against GM crops, or whaling, or nuclear power, you're supposed to go: 'Well, they must know what they're talking about. They're sincere, and they're not government stooges – they're real people and they care.' Greenpeace's sanctification in the public imagination is not dissimilar to the one achieved by the Princess of Wales during that scary bout of national hysteria after her death. To criticise Greenpeace is tantamount to saying: 'I'm a total bastard who hates the world, doesn't understand anything and likes torturing kittens – especially the really cute ones with mismatching eyes like you see on those charming kitten calendars.'

But quite the scariest thing about Greenpeace is that it's not at all the disinterested, nature-loving charity it pretends to be. Sure it cares about the environment. But what it cares about at least as much is raising ever larger amounts of money so as to expand its power base. The way it does this, as most charities do, is by extravagant publicity stunts. And if generating publicity means playing fast and loose with the truth ... Well, if you can get away with it, why the hell not?

Greenpeace's greatest fundraising stunt was also its most shabbily dishonest moment. In 1995, it launched a noisy campaign against Shell's plans to dispose of a disused oil rig – *Brent Spar* – by sinking it in the waters of the mid-Atlantic. As the Natural Environmental Research Council subsequently confirmed, this was by far the most eco-friendly option and, as most shipwrecks do, would have provided an ideal habitat for numerous varieties of marine life. But Greenpeace cared less about the facts than the publicity value. Its successful European boycott of Shell petrol stations generated acres of newspaper coverage, while shots of its plucky young eco-warriors in their tiny inflatables harassing the tugs towing the rig appeared on countless TV news bulletins. Many of Greenpeace's claims – notably that the rig was full of toxic residues – were inaccurate. But the charity's distortions won it the propaganda war and that was the important thing: Shell was bullied into disposing of the rig elsewhere.

A decade earlier when its ship *Rainbow Warrior* was blown up by French saboteurs in New Zealand, Greenpeace deliberately sank it offshore, claiming it would make an artificial reef ideal for marine life. One rule for hateful capitalist multinational oil firms, then; quite another for high-minded eco-heroes.

Hardy, Jeremy (see also Steel, Mark)

Comedian whose humour you really need to be a Radio 4 commissioning editor to get.

Like a Japanese soldier in the remote Philippine jungle who hasn't yet realised that the Second World War is over, so Hardy is still under the sad delusion the miners are on strike, the hated Thatch is still in power, Troops should be Out of Northern Ireland and that what the country needs to sort out its problems is a healthy dose of honest-to-goodness, unreconstructed Marxism.

Hate crime

So if a murderer kills me because I won't give him my wallet or I looked at him in a funny way or he doesn't like my poncy accent, that's not nearly as bad as if he kills someone else for being black or gay? Yes, this is the British law as it now stands. Thanks to the brilliant new, buy-up-more-minority-votes 'hate crime' legislation introduced by New Labour, my life as a white heterosexual is valued – in murder-sentencing terms – at roughly 50 per cent less than those of my gay or ethnic minority neighbours.

Orwell had a name for this: 'thought crime'. Except, of course, when he invented it he thought he was just satirising the sort of thing that happens in a totalitarian state – not in a liberal democracy.

Health And Safety (see also Ladders, People Falling Off)

'Everything that's fun in life is dangerous . . . And everything that isn't fun is dangerous too. It is impossible to be alive and safe.'
P. J. O'Rourke

We're all going to die. Accidents do happen. By about the age of ten, even the thickest among us have grasped these self-evident truths. All of us, that is, save the lame brains of the health and safety industry. Until these deranged idealists can absolutely guarantee that no one is hurt or injured in any way whatsoever ever again, they seem to think, then their work on this earth can never be considered done.

Health and safety means stories like these:

Paper napkins in Tewkesbury, Gloucestershire being withdrawn by the council from the meals-on-wheels service for fear that pensioners and disabled people might choke on them.

The BBC issuing staff with 'Revolving Security Door User Instructions' after a woman caught her foot in the doors at BBC Birmingham.

Moscow State Circus being warned in July 2003 that any acrobat performing at a height above that of the average step-ladder would have to wear a hard hat or risk losing its insurance cover.

Norwich City Council planning to chop down twenty horse chestnut trees lest passers-by sustain head injuries from sticks thrown by children to knock down conkers.

Gardeners at Cheltenham Council being banned from planting pansies under town-centre trees because workers digging with trowels risked spraining their wrists in the root-filled soil.

A St George's Day patriotic fry-up in Bromham, Wiltshire being cancelled by the council because it contravened guidelines that 'protein-based foods' should only be prepared by volunteers with 'proper training'. A seventy-three-year-old man being thrown off a Cardiff bus because he was carrying a tin of paint which the driver deemed a 'hazardous article'.

Whom should we blame for this never-ending stream of life-ruining misery? Well the EU, obviously, for that's where all these health and safety directives come from. But, please, let's not forget to hate and despise also all those petty officials and council jobsworths who work so tirelessly to enforce them. Elf 'n' Safety has become their legal- and authoritative-sounding version of 'the computer says "No"': a way of inflicting their stubborn grey miserableness on the world without needing to bother with tedious details like logic, courtesy, fairness, effort, decency or common sense. Nor should we miss the chance to have a dig at David Aaronovitch, tireless defender of Health and Safety regulations on the grounds that in 1972, no fewer than eight brewery workers were roasted in hop kilns or accidentally turned into beer, whereas the latest figure was only three, which just goes to show . . . etc. (NB this isn't a real fact. But it's the sort of thing he does go on about to prove why Health and Safety has made our lives immeasurably better.)

Really, though, the people we ought most to blame for this nonsense are ourselves. Once, though a tiny island, we made ourselves great and conquered the world by dint of sheer will and devil-may-care courage ('Always attack' was Nelson's motto). Now we have grown so ashamed of our past and so morally enfeebled, we have apparently decided that the nations we once trashed on the battlefield and blasted off the high seas should now be free to trample all over us with their pettifogging directives governing every aspect of our lives from how we seat our children in cars to how we repair our pipe organs.

Health and Safety? It's no more than we ruddy deserve.

Heath, Ted

C***.

History

Ever wondered why kids no longer know even the date of the Battle of Hastings? It's because the national curriculum doesn't allow history teachers to teach history any more – only historiography. Historiography dispenses with all that old-fashioned nonsense like kings and queens and dates and battles and key events. Instead, it introduces children to the thing that matters most about our past: that it is the ever-changing summation of a multiplicity of competitive viewpoints which render all attempts at objectivity ultimately meaningless.

Confused? Not half as confused as the poor little buggers who have to study this post-modern gibberish. Instead of sitting back and listening while their teacher regales them with all history's juicy bits – Edward II with his poker-up-the-bottom; the Duke of Clarence drowning in a butt of malmsey; Sir Francis Drake capturing a Spanish galleon whose name *Cacafuego* doesn't mean 'spit fire', class, it means 'shit fire', etc. – they're now supposed to find it out for themselves.

Using a modish technique called the 'discovery method', kids are supposed to treat history not as a series of well-defined events but as a string of nebulous, ever-shifting problems and mysteries which they personally must solve. And it's no good reading it all up in a reliable history primer because schools don't use that sort of thing any more. Instead, the in textbooks are more like cut-and-paste collages of bitsy excerpts from random historical writings: the Fire of London, say, as described by Samuel Pepys; by his cleaning lady; by a modern fire prevention officer; by the *Sun*'s TV critic reviewing a programme about the Fire of London; by a disabled Albanian primary schoolgirl writing about the event from the imaginary viewpoint of a flea on the back of a dying plague rat.

Trendy educationalists think all this is great. It fits in perfectly with their groovy theories that children only learn if they teach themselves, and that things like facts and retentive memories don't matter any more now that you look everything up on the internet.

But where does that leave the rest of us? Screamingly frustrated. We know how important history is to our cultural identity and we yearn for it to be taught in the proper, old-fashioned way. So how come the history teaching method EVERYBODY wants – apart from a handful of left-wing theorists – has been replaced by one that no one likes and which doesn't work? It would be nice to think that future historians could tell us. Except, the way things are going, there probably won't be any.

Home Information Pack

Ingenious torture scheme devised by John Prescott (*qv*) to punish people for moving house. Home sellers were originally supposed to waste hundreds of pounds on a compulsory inspection report which no serious buyer would have bothered to use because they would have commissioned their own survey anyway. A government spokesman claimed that HIPs would speed up housing transactions by shifting some of the cost from buyer to seller, reducing the scope for gazumping and making sure fewer deals fell through. But then when Prescott fell out of favour, the project was watered down – the compulsory inspection report is now voluntary – in belated acknowledgement that, yes, like all Prescott's other political ideas it was monstrously, unbelievably crap.

Hothousing (see also Broad Social Mix)

Excuse routinely used by impoverished middle-class parents to cover up their shame and embarrassment at not being able to afford to give their children a decent education. 'Ah, yes, but the reason Saint Paul's gets such incredible results is that it's just an exam factory. With all that hothousing, the poor children don't have any time to develop their personalities...' Also comes in handy when your children fail to get into one of those uncharacteristically academic state schools where there are fifteen applications for every place. 'Well, of course, I'm frankly relieved that little Johnny didn't get in. I'd much rather have him turn out a rounded individual than one of those hothoused automatons...'

Human Rights

Food, shelter, warmth and – what was the other one? Oh, yeah, that's it: the right to hijack a planeload of terrified Afghans, fly to Britain and live there indefinitely at taxpayers' expense because, hey, Afghanistan's scary, full of people who hijack planes and stuff.

Then there's the right to sue your school because you're the teacher and the chair you've been given makes embarrassing farty noises. And the right to fly over from Nigeria with a dicky heart and get a free one on the NHS (qv). And the right to rape someone, then get released on parole so that you're free to make a proper job of it and murder your next victim instead.

Blimey, who would have thought there were so many human rights out there? No wonder our lawyers are kept so busy fighting the good fight for the inalienable right of terrorists, ambulance-chasers, vexatious litigants, chippy minorities, difficult school-children, angry prisoners, losers, second-raters and criminals to get away with murder while the rest of us look on stunned and shout: 'Hang on a second. What about MY human rights?'

It would be nice to blame the Human Rights Act (HRA) introduced by Mr Blair and his barrister chums in the wave of smug, more-work-for-the-lawyers (*qv*) do-goodery that followed his election in 1997. But actually, even if the HRA were abolished tomorrow, we would still be facing the same old nonsense from the courts in Strasbourg which – as signatories of the European Convention on Human Rights – we're obliged by law to take more seriously than any court in Britain.

But what are human rights? The problem is, nobody knows, which leaves the field wide open for lawyers to interpret them any way they please and for troublemakers to take legal action on the barmiest of pretexts. Bothered by the fact that there isn't a colour TV in your prison cell? Don't much fancy wearing your school uniform? Simple: just claim your human rights have been abused and the courts will take your complaint as seriously as if your wife and children had just been murdered, or you'd been heard uttering a racist remark.

Where it gets even trickier is that our individual human rights seem to conflict with so many others' human rights. My human right to privacy, for example, may lead me to grow the *leylandii* hedge which, in turn, imposes on your human right not to have all your sunlight stolen by my vile two-feet-a-year's growth of coniferous disaster zone. Also, if human rights really are universal and absolute, how does that fit in with the privileges traditionally afforded with British citizenship? What right have we to stop an illegal immigrant, or a legal one for that matter, coming over here and claiming their right to free health care, shelter and schooling?

If only we'd listened to Jeremy Bentham, the eighteenth-century philosopher who recognised early on that human rights – 'natural rights' as he called them – were 'nonsense upon stilts'.

Yes, he appreciated that they were a nice idea in theory. But just because something ought to be the case (there are 'reasons for wishing there were such a thing as rights', he said) doesn't mean it actually is the case: 'Hunger is not bread,' he explained. Unless, he might have added, you work for Matrix Chambers.

Hung Out To Dry

Who'd want to join the army these days? Your old mates are all safely at home – shagging, boozing, taking drugs, playing on their Gameboys, doing whatever they damn well please – while you're on patrol in Iraq or Afghanistan, cramped, sweating and perpetually on edge inside a vehicle with sides so thin they could scarcely stop a bullet, let alone a rocket-propelled grenade (RPG) or one of those hideous new directional charges that can tear through an armoured personnel carrier (APC) like a hot knife through butter and turn everyone inside into strawberry jam. All this you accept – it's part of the job – but what's much, much harder to bear is that at the slightest slip up you could end up being court-martialled, losing your job and spending what's left of the youth you voluntarily gave up for Queen and Country doing time at Her Majesty's Pleasure.

Where once you would have been tried by your peers – fellow soldiers and officers who understood the peculiar exigencies of combat – you are now increasingly likely to be prosecuted according to the values of civilian courts by people who know a great deal about oppressed minorities' human rights but very little about what it's like to be sitting next to your best mate when he has his leg taken off by an Improvised Explosive Device (IED) while men dressed as civilians spray you with AK47s from behind a screen of women and children.

Why has this happened? Partly because in Tony Blair's holy

mission to heal the world, the soldiers implementing his 'ethical' foreign policy are expected to behave in the heat of combat with a restraint and sensitivity which would challenge a social worker on a quiet afternoon in Tunbridge Wells. After PR disasters like Abu Ghraib, our government is pathetically eager to appease Muslim grievance by showing itself to be 'fair' and 'even-handed'. And what better way of doing so than hanging a few hapless squaddies out to dry?

Imagine what this does to morale. You're on patrol in a war zone – keyed up, nervous and extremely vulnerable – yet you're burdened by rules of engagement which mean it's almost safer to risk being shot than to fire at the enemy. The opposition exploit this to the full: firing from mosques; firing from crowds of civilians; dropping their weapons the instant British soldiers return fire, the more easily to have them prosecuted for firing on unarmed men.

If this is how we intend to fight our wars in the future, our chances of winning are going to be very small indeed.

Hunting

'It isn't mere convention. Everyone can see that the people who hunt are the right people and the people that don't are the wrong ones.'
G. B. Shaw, Heartbreak House.

Here are five reasons I never once heard being advanced by the Countryside Alliance in defence of hunting.

1. The kit's fab, like an eighteenth-century gentleman's.
2. Apart from darts, it's the only sport where being pissed is virtually compulsory.
3. The atmosphere and camaraderie are like being at a warehouse rave in the days when everyone was 'on one'.

4. It feels a bit like doing acid, with the difference that it's really, actually happening.
5. It's as enjoyable as sex, only it lasts four hours longer.

Sure there are lots of other sound arguments too: the preservation of rural livelihoods; the binding of communities; the maintenance of tradition; vermin control; and so on. But I'm not sure how terribly compelling they are, now that we're dominated by a smug urban majority which honestly couldn't give a stuff one way or another what happens to a few yokels in the sticks.

The fun side of hunting, on the other hand, is something with which most of us can identify: it's fast; it's scary; it's incredibly dangerous. You're riding on top of one wild animal (horses go barmy when they hunt) in mad pursuit of another, rarely with the foggiest idea what lies ahead or round the next bend. There's a bit of skill involved, a bit of luck and a lot of pure adrenaline. And because it's so risky, you all tend to look after one another and think about one another's needs in a way that has become all too rare in this age of me, me, me.

Whether you find a fox is almost immaterial. And if you do, so what, he almost always gets away. And if he doesn't, well tough, that's nature: red in tooth and claw. And if you think, somehow, that man has risen above all that, well just look at Rwanda, Iraq, Afghanistan, the Congo, the two World Wars ... Oh, and do be sure to remember the name of the man responsible for banning hunting in Germany on grounds of cruelty: Adolf Hitler.

I

'I don't mind paying a bit more in taxes if it means greater social justice/a better health service/education system . . .'

If that's what you feel, mate, go right ahead. Put a kid from the council estate through Eton. Fund your cleaning lady's sex change op. End world poverty. Do what you like: it's your money. And so long as it's just your money you're talking about it, we don't mind one bit.

But, when you start talking about increased taxes, you're no longer talking about just your money, are you? You're talking about our money, too. You're saying: 'If I'm so comfortably smug in my Clerkenwell warehouse apartment with my Croatian investment villa and my state-pensioned job in a government quango that I can afford to throw away a bit more of my dosh, that must mean everyone else can afford it too.' Which isn't right, at all. For one thing, after a decade's stealth taxes from Gordon Brown, a lot of us are skint. For another, maybe we've come to the conclusion that increased taxation only leads to more waste, bureaucracy, state control and jobs for pillocks like you. And for yet another, if we ever did have the dosh, maybe we'd rather spend it on private healthcare, or a holiday, or *Medal Of Honor VI*, or an internet porn subscription, or whatever the hell we like. OUR MONEY. NOT YOURS. Got that?

Icons Online

England, ah, England. The sound of leather on willow; the lengthening shadows across the village green; warm beer; cream teas; and then, come winter, the music of the hunt in full cry – and the hunt saboteurs with their video cameras, their balaclavas and their jaunty iron bars.

But hold on a moment. What are the sabs doing here? I thought we were dwelling languorously on all those things that make England so wonderfully, quintessentially English. You'd need a pretty warped sense of priorities to extend that category to include a bunch of snarling, cam-jacketed militants from the animal rights lobby.

Yet this is just what has happened at Icons Online – the state-sponsored propaganda website funded by you, the taxpayer, to the tune of £1 million – which has decided to include in its list of English icons a category called 'Foxhunting and the Ban'.

'In England, whenever images of horses and hounds come to mind, so too, inevitably do images of hunt saboteurs and scuffles with the police,' claimed the website's managing director Jerry Doyle, bizarrely. 'We can't ignore the fact that tea cloths, place mats and paintings the world over depict hunting pinks and that they are identified with this country in a particular kind of way. But it is a hugely emotive issue and we want to be fair and to cover both sides of the debate.'

Please can we have our one million quid back? Now.

Immigration

Tried using the bus recently? Or getting an appointment to see your doctor? Or finding a space in your local primary school? Or an hour of the day or a section of road where the traffic isn't nose to tail? Britain is getting noticeably more crowded, it's been going on for quite some time and yet until very recently we were all expected to act like you do when someone farts in the lift – keep a straight face and pretend it hasn't happened.

Apparently this is all because of a speech made by Enoch Powell nearly forty years ago. Never mind what it actually said – hardly anyone has ever read it – it's just one of those known facts that it was called the 'Rivers Of Blood' speech, that it was very, very bad and that it automatically makes anyone who so much as thinks about raising the subject of immigration a complete and utter racist bastard.

Really though, why is it wrong to talk about immigration? It's not as though Britain has limitless, Siberian-sized wastelands crying out to be populated. Neither is it as though the only people who don't want immigration are the snooty white people, whereas all the black, brown and yellow ones are going: 'Yes. Come on in, everybody. We hate open spaces! We like being crushed!' Immigration, surely, is a British issue rather than a specifically Anglo-Saxon one.

And it really is of pressing concern. Britain is twice as crowded as Germany, four times as crowded as France and twelve times as crowded as the US. Net immigration is running at nearly 350,000 a year, with immigrants now accounting for 83 per cent of our population growth. By 2031, according to government projections, the immigrant population will have increased by six million, the equivalent of six Birminghams. But that's just the official guesstimate. Not even the laughably incompetent Immigration and Nationality Directorate has a clue what the true figure is, because so many immigrants arrive illegally. According to MigrationWatch, the UK's illegal immigrant population in 2006 was around 750,000.

Yet, for some, these aren't facts we should ever have been

allowed to know. When retired diplomat Sir Andrew Green founded MigrationWatch — an avowedly non-partisan body designed purely to raise public awareness of immigration levels to Britain — it was dismissed by the *Independent* as a 'nasty little outfit with a distinctly unpleasant agenda'.

There are lots of mysteries about modern Britain: why the wind-farm lobby has triumphed despite the overwhelming evidence that wind farms are rubbish; why we don't pull out of the EU; why New Labour has managed to stay in power for so long; why management consultants? But surely the greatest mystery of all is this: how could it be that for the four decades after 'Rivers of Blood' a tiny minority of *bien-pensants* was able to so terrify the majority that never once did they dare seriously discuss the issue closest to their hearts — the Britishness of the British?

Impossibility of enjoying rock gigs at indoor venues now that you're no longer able to fire up your spliff when the really good bit comes, The

Live rock music isn't the same without drugs. No matter how great the euphoric rush you get at the point in the set when your favourite band has waded through the preliminary filler and is finally playing the opening bars of *The Song You Really Wanted To Hear*, it's not going to be nearly as intense without the first hit of that fat spliff you prepared earlier to enhance this very moment.

Of course, in theory, smoking joints was never allowed in public rock venues. But at least in the old days you could sneak your spliff in past the door inspection by hiding it at the bottom of your rolling baccie, wade towards the middle of the crowd — whence the bouncers would have difficulty removing you even if they wanted to – and rely on the general smoky fug, and the fact that lots of other people were smoking joints too, to protect you from being caught.

Now, unfortunately, that's not a viable option. It's not the smoking of a joint that threatens to have you thrown out of the venue. It's the very fact that you're smoking at all. A blanket ban on smoking is much easier to enforce than one which relies on the bouncers' ability to discern whether your cigarette contains something illicit.

And so another fine tradition bites the dust. Gigs will become that little bit less exciting. The music will become marginally less enjoyable – that of bands like Mogwai and Ian Brown, especially. Outdoor music events will become more popular than ever because they will be the only place left where you can hear rock music as it was meant to be heard – i.e. stoned. And maybe two, possibly three, or even four people fewer per year will die of smoking-related illnesses. If this is progress, let's all kill ourselves now. (See also, Smoking, Numerous Arguments In Favour Of, The)

Inappropriate (see also Judgemental)

Slimy euphemism – especially popular with psychotherapists – for 'wrong'. This is symptomatic of a new strain of thinking in our godless, post-moral, culturally relativistic age which has it that no one any longer has a right to judge anyone else's behaviour according to absolute moral standards. 'There is no such thing as right or wrong but thinking makes it so,' as Hamlet might have put it were he alive today and running a lucrative psychotherapy practice in North London.

Investment

Weaselly New Labour euphemism designed to make wasteful state expenditure on pointless projects sound like a desirable and profitable thing.

Iraq

Should we have gone in or shouldn't we? Was Saddam Hussein's Kurd-gassing, Marsh-Arab-destroying, Shia-massacring, feeding-the-opposition-alive-into-mincing-machine tyranny preferable to the civil-war chaos that has replaced it? Have fewer or more people died as a result of the Allied intervention? Were there really ever any weapons of mass destruction? Was it legal?

We can debate all these things till hell freezes over or the polar ice caps melt and still we'll never reach a satisfactory conclusion. But surely there's at least one basic fact we ought all to agree on: we're not there because we're evil.

Maybe we went in to safeguard our oil supply (see Oil, It's All About); maybe because of an ambitious Neo-Con plan to encourage democracy to spread through the Middle East; maybe we did it out of humanitarian concern for Saddam's suffering people; maybe we really did believe that Saddam posed a nuclear, chemical or biological threat to the region. Who cares? They're all sound enough reasons. They're all in the interests of a more stable, peaceful, civilised world. Had it worked out, we would have all stood to benefit, whether it was conducted in 'our name' or no. That's what foreign policy is all about: enlightened self-interest.

So why is it that whenever we talk about Iraq these days our consensus view differs so little from the one on the Arab street and among Islamist propaganda organisations that we might as well all give up now and join the Baghdad branch of al-Qaeda?

We talk of the Allied 'occupation'. We ignore all the suicide bombs and booby traps, and the dozens of ordinary Iraqis and Allied soldiers killed by terrorists and insurgents, but we home in like Predator spy drones on any news story which shows our troops in a bad light. We appear genuinely to believe that the Allies' primary purpose in Iraq is to leech its natural resources and go round beating up, abusing and killing its populace for the sheer bloody hell of it.

Isn't there something we're forgetting here? Iraq is a dump. It's ugly, it's dangerous, it's expensive, it's unpopular – there's no short- or even medium-term profit in it. The only conceivable reason for our still being there, in other words, is that some of us still think it's our moral duty. This may be stupid of us, but if this makes us the bad guys then I'm Robert Fisk's right testicle.

J

Jenkins, Woy (see also Heath, Ted)

Fat, Welsh, Europhile snob with fake posh accent and affected claret habit now being roasted on a spit in the hottest part of hell for having invented the phrase: 'Cewebwate diversity.'

Judgemental (see also Prejudice)

'Lacks judgement'. In the days when Britain still counted for something, this was a serious deficiency. It meant you were likely to hang out with rackety friends who'd get you into all sorts of dreadful scrapes; it meant you were unfit to run a business or take care of your family; it meant that when you were put in charge of a column of 1,000 men armed with rifles and gatling guns, the chances were you'd all end up being massacred by half-a-dozen natives armed with spears.

And so it has been since at least the days of Aristotle and the invention of empiricism and classification: judgement has been prized in the Western world as the hallmark of maturity and wisdom. Good judgement is a sign that you have studied the world, marked its lessons well, and formed the ability to make sound decisions based on your accumulated experience. Bad judgement is for fools. No judgement is for the spineless, the childish and the mentally deficient.

But not any more, apparently. In its latest usage, 'judgement' has been transformed from a desirable attribute into an essentially malign one. Being 'judgemental' we are told — especially by psychotherapists (see also Inappropriate) — is something we should try whenever possible not to be. If we spent less time judging people and more time empathising with them, the world would be a considerably less messed-up place. Or so the theory runs.

The major flaw in the non-judgemental theory is that, when taken to its logical extreme, it exposes us to all kinds of unnecessary risk. How ever are we to avoid being conned by con men, raped by rapists or murdered by murderers if we're so busy striving to look for the best in people that we cast aside all judgement and throw ourselves at the mercy of an imaginary benign providence?

To be judgemental is not to err. It's a sign of being a discriminating (see Discrimination) human being.

K

Kilimanjaro

What the eco lobby doesn't tell you about its star mountain-in-peril is that Hemingway's magnificent snowy ice cap has been melting for ages – long before man-made-global-warming supposedly kicked in. It suffered its most dramatic glacial melt between 1912 and 1953. Unfortunately the world in that period was being distracted by trivia like the two world wars and was consequently unable to give this catastrophic problem the hand-wringing attention it properly deserved.

Kyoto Protocol (see also Global Warming)

If there's one thing everyone knows about global warming, it's that the only way we can possibly avert the greatest disaster in the history of mankind is for us all to sign up to the Kyoto Protocol. Never mind what the Kyoto Protocol means, or who invented it on what shaky scientific grounds, or how much it will cost, or whether it will make the blindest bit of difference. Just sign it, quick, before the ice caps melt and we all drown.

For those who care about the tiny details, though, there are at least two enormous things wrong with the Kyoto Protocol. The first is how risibly little effect it will have on global warming. Suppose every signatory – including the United States – were to implement its proposals, that would still only reduce the world's surface temperature by 0.07°C (0.13°F) in fifty years. And even that, of course, is an impossible dream since none of its signatories, not even the most obsessively green ones, is expected to meet the protocol's modest emissions reductions. And even if, by some miracle, they all did suddenly turn around and summon up the economy-wreaking zeal needed to implement Kyoto's demands, all their noble intentions would be rendered worthless by the carbon emissions of all those countries that haven't signed up to Kyoto, notably China.

The second enormous thing wrong with Kyoto is that it is insanely, cripplingly expensive. If Kyoto were implemented tomorrow, it might postpone the effects of global warming by six years – i.e. we'd get in 2106 the temperature we might otherwise have got in 2100 – at a cost to the world economy per annum of $150 billion. Yet as Bjørn 'Skeptical Environmentalist' Lomborg (qv) has pointed out, for just one year's worth of that wasted money we could provide clean drinking water and sanitation for every person on the planet. Which do we value more highly: millions of human lives or the neuroses of green scaremongers?

Labour MPs Who Send Their Children To Private School

Look, of course we'd all send our children to private school if we had half the chance: how else are we going to guarantee them a decent education now that the state system is so royally, comprehensively and irredeemably knackered?

No longer are the better state schools permitted to select prospective pupils by examination or parental interview because this – heaven forfend – might discriminate in favour of bright ones with caring parents who've instilled in them a bit of discipline and a desire to work. No longer can state schools get rid of disruptive pupils because, apparently, work-shy thugs are a problem that should be shared round equally rather than parcelled off to the sort of specialist schools that know how to deal with them. No longer are the exams that state school children do worth taking anyway, because the system's so corrupt and the currency is so debased, that only by submitting to a voluntary lobotomy can you expect to leave school these days with fewer than twenty A*s. No longer are state schools capable of giving an education worth the name, because all they care about is league tables, which just mean endlessly revised coursework and a reluctance to diverge even slightly from the narrow, idiot-friendly, dumbed-down syllabus. No longer do state schools do any sport a) because it's competitive, b) because of health and safety and insurance issues and c) because they've sold off all their playing fields anyway.

So, yes, any parent who didn't take the private school option if they had the money could scarcely be considered to have done their duty as a sane, healthy, decent human being.

Except that is, for one notable exception. Suppose you were an MP who belonged to the very political party and the very government whose policies and ideology had created this educational mess in the first place: if you were to send your child to private school and give it the first-class education you had denied so many others, well, that would make you someone, would it not, for whom hanging was far, FAR too good?

Ladders, People Falling Off (see also Health And Safety)

Police in Rochdale refused to inspect damage to a smashed stained-glass window after a break-in at a church because they did not have specialist 'ladder training'. Your TV aerial's on the blink, your roof's leaking, your gutter's blocked and you'd love to be able to get someone out to change that out-of-reach bulb on the lamp in the church hall. But can you find anyone to help? Course not. Health 'n' Safety, innit.

David Aaronovitch (*qv*) argues that in 2004 no fewer than thirteen people were killed falling off ladders, with another 1,200 injured, and it's to protect people like them that our health and safety regulations need to be so stringent and intrusive.

But surely no amount of well-meaning legislation is going to affect the randomness and cruelty of fate?

As for those people who fell off their ladders – they were all victims of what's known in the trade as 'bad luck'. They knew the risks, as we all do when we climb up tall, narrow, wobbly structures with shaky bases and rungs that could collapse at any second. And I'll bet if, before their falls, you'd asked them their views on the obscene lengths to which we all have to go to keep in tune with health and safety these days, they would have said the same: 'Cheers, mate, but I'd rather take my chances.'

Language Teaching In Schools (see also Grade Inflation)

Our education system hasn't really dumbed down, its apologists claim: it has just evolved a form of learning more in tune with the modern age. So, instead of being crammed with facts – times tables, grammar, the periodic table – as their put-upon forebears were, today's children are offered the chance to develop the analytical and creative parts of their brain, and thus emerge far more intellectually rounded.

To appreciate what utter rot this is, consider the decline in language teaching. In the old days, when you studied, say, French to O level standard, you emerged with a reasonable grasp of the grammar – and the ability to make yourself understood on your next family holiday in Brittany. By the time you'd done the A level, you would emerge able to speak the language with some fluency, with a sound knowledge of the grammar, and a familiarity with half-a-dozen plays by Molière, some Racine, some Corneille – giving you just the intellectual grounding you needed if you wanted to carry on studying the subject at university.

But now look what's happened. Today it is fully possible to get an A at French A level while yet being quite unable to speak the language, or understand the grammar, or read any of its great works of literature.

Are our children better off as a result of not having being forced to endure old-school learning-by-rote?

Well, not if you're old fashioned enough to think that the point of learning a language is to learn the language, no.

Lawyers

'Kill all the lawyers,' Shakespeare famously said but that's not what he wrote in his first draft. Problem was, 'Hange, drawe and quarter all ye lawyers, stampe on theyre heades and dance for ioye for verily they are ye cockroaches of ye earthe and no punishment is too vile for them,' didn't quite scan. Astonishing, though, the man's perspicacity – given that human rights and personal injuries lawyers hadn't even been invented back then.

Yes, yes, I know some lawyers who are my friends, and nice. Probably you know some lawyers who are that way too. In no wise, though, should this distract us from the essential truth about the legal profession: that it combines the morals of the prostitute and the cynicism of the mercenary with the arrogant sanctimon-iousness of the Taliban.

Try pressing a lawyer on whether they think, say, the murderer really did or didn't do it. They won't say. They don't care. They're genuinely not interested. All that matters to them is whether or not the crime's alleged perpetrator was or wasn't found 'guilty under law'. For them, you see, the criminal justice system has absolutely nothing to do with right or wrong. It's about due process. About whether they and all their other mates in wigs followed the right procedures, sucked up to the presiding judge at the right moments, picked up the police on all the evidential inconsistencies, got their guilty-as-sin client off on the right technicality, that sort of thing. What matters to them is the 'majesty of the law'.

Of course one can perfectly well understand why lawyers think this way. They have to, it's their job. In any given case, there's only a fifty/fifty chance that they'll be representing the good side (whichever that is: wronged innocent or wholly justified CPS) so, clearly, it's quite important that they feel comfortable about endorsing evil.

What's so galling though, is that they'll never admit it. You won't hear a lawyer saying: 'You're right. We're completely amoral. We'll represent any cause, no matter how repellant, so long as we're paid enough, because, hey, that's what lawyers are like.' They actually believe in their warped imaginations that they have a claim to the moral high ground; that even as they make more and more work for themselves, leeching off society's misfortunes and claiming a greater and greater share of our money, they are genuinely making the world a better, more civilised place.

This moral blindness explains why so many lawyers vote Labour. They simply can't see the inconsistency between enjoying all the trappings of their £300,000-plus salaries, while yet supporting the party which would seek to deny that luxury to those of us who had the misfortune not to become lawyers ourselves.

Left Wing (see also Right Wing)

Left-wingers are: devil-may-care; good in bed; raffishly tousled; cool; sexy. They: sympathise with the underdog; hate injustice; respect the working class and people of all races and creeds, regardless of looks, physical ability or gender; nurture the environment; have great taste in music; oppose violence; loathe inequality; are kind to children and to small furry animals with lovely bright eyes and darling floppy ears and expressions on their sweet pink little mouths you could almost mistake for a human smile.

All of which goes to prove how incredibly principled right-wing people are. If they wanted to, they could choose the political affiliation which miraculously confers on them all these wondrous things. But they don't, because for right-wingers truth is more important than social convenience.

Litter (see also Diwali; Anti-Racism; Environment, The; Seacole, Mary)

Principal topic at all state primary schools.

Little Englander

(n.) Idiot who stubbornly refuses to accept that higher taxes, greater bureaucracy, loss of national sovereignty and the introduction of wave upon wave of pointless, meddling, irritating, pettifogging regulations are just what Britain needs.

One of the European Union Project's greatest victories has been linguistic. Helped by its cheerleaders in the liberal media – the *Independent*, the *Guardian*, and most especially the BBC – the Project has successfully managed to portray anyone who disagrees with its aims as either a bigot or a crazed extremist. 'Little Englander', 'swivel-eyed', 'hysterical' and 'fanatical' are among the tags routinely used to dismiss any public figure who expresses doubts about the Project. Indeed, as Christopher Booker and Richard North point out in their forensic dissection of EU malpractice – *The Great Deception* – the terms 'europhobe' and 'europhile' are inherently biased towards the pro-EU position. To be a '-phobe' of something is to be negative, closed-minded, fearful, suspicious. To be a '-phile', on the other hand, is evidence of bonhomie, love and goodwill. Even more helpful to the Project's cause is the way 'Europe' is commonly used as shorthand for 'European Union', as if the two concepts were interchangeable. So, if you're 'anti-Europe' you're not merely against the idea of being ruled by a body of democratically unaccountable supranational technocrats, you're also, by inference, against risotto *alla seppia*, BMWs, the Eiffel Tower, the Prado, olive groves on a Greek island with a donkey standing underneath, Belgian chocolate, the Côte d'Azur . . . And what kind of nutter would you have to be to reject all that?

Live Aid (see also Rock Stars)

Fund-raising event which helps needy African dictators enlarge their fleets of Mercedes, while simultaneously enabling white, middle-class people to demonstrate conspicuous compassion.

Livingstone, Ken

Elected leader of the Greater London Council; elected a Labour MP; twice elected Mayor of London. A pretty overwhelming argument against the whole concept of democracy, then.

Lobsters, boiling alive (see Foie Gras)

Lomborg, Bjørn

Lomborg is the lefty tree-hugger and Greenpeace member who went over to the Dark Side with a shocking new theory: that we're not, after all, about to be wiped out by acid rain/nuclear waste/melting polar ice caps/global warming/industrial effluvia/evil capitalists' wanton disregard of the eco-system; that in fact, all things considered, the earth's in pretty good shape.

Whether you choose to believe him or not, you might at least be given pause by the green lobby's extraordinary response. Instead of trying to engage with his argument – quite tricky, given that the statistics he analyses in his book *The Skeptical Environmentalist* are exactly the same ones used by organisations such as Greenpeace and the World Wildlife Fund (WWF) – both have attacked him personally. He has been called 'antichrist', vilified *ad hominem* in numerous science journals, denounced as 'unscientific' by an *ad hoc* committee calling itself the Danish Committees On Scientific Dishonesty and had a custard pie thrown in his face by an eco-campaigner at an Oxford book signing.

Maths A Level (see also Grade Inflation)

If you got a grade B in your 2005 Maths A Level you've nothing to crow about. According to research by the think tank Reform, in 1988 you would only have got yourself a grade E.

Mayor Of LondON (see also Livingstone, Ken)

Which is it that irks the most, I wonder? The way Ken's marketing people have chosen, for no apparent reason, to single out that second 'ON' in red, capital letters so that every time you see it your internal reading voice goes 'LondON' in an annoying and pointless way? Or the propagandistic notion implicit in these advertising posters that Ken Livingstone is a kindly, avuncular figure whose only delight is to sit in his office dreaming up firework displays, rock concerts, poetry galas, anti-racism festivals and suchlike for the edification and amusement of his beloved metropolis?

Surely the whole point of having been born in Britain rather than, say, Kim Il Sung's North Korea, Enver Hoxha's Albania or Saddam Hussein's Iraq, is that crackpot personality cults like this ought to be a distant nightmare.

Media Studies

Research has shown that doing media studies at uni (*qv*) actually results in your earning less money, on average, than if you'd never gone to university at all. I work in the media and I can confirm this. We never give jobs to media studies graduates if we can help it. We hand them out to our mates who were in our colleges at Oxford or Cambridge instead.

Melting Pot

Desperate excuse trotted out by middle-class homeowners who can't afford to live anywhere posh as to why they've 'chosen' to live on the fringes of a crack-ridden ghetto. As in: 'Yes, well we did look at Wandsworth and Clapham, obviously, but I'm afraid we found them a little too tame. Now that's never something you could say, living here, just off Coldharbour Lane. The ackee fruit! The goat curry! The sheer vibrancy of it all. It's a real melting pot.'

Military Hospitals

We barely have one left: the others were all abandoned because of MOD cheeseparing. Which is why British soldiers in action no longer hope for the 'Blighty wound' that will get them safely home. What they want is a 'Boche wound' – an injury to the head which will get them sent to the excellent US military neurological hospital in Ramstein, Germany. Better the risk of permanent brain damage, they reason, than the horror of being shipped from the battlefield to some crummy British NHS hospital ward where on one side of them they've got an incontinent geriatric, on the other a mental health patient, and coming through the door past the non-existent security system a vindictive Islamist bent on exacting revenge for what's been happening to his 'brothers' in Iraq and Afghanistan.

Millennium Bug

What happened, eh? It was supposed to wipe out our economy, unless we acted quickly, this terrible electronic bug which was apparently going to be created by our computers' inability to comprehend that the year 2000 had finally arrived.

But it didn't and it was never going to. It was just a brilliant conspiracy theory dreamed up in a collaboration between panicky, techno-illiterate ministers delighted to have an opportunity to show themselves up to speed with the modern world, newspaper editors in search of a suitably apocalyptic yet grown-up-sounding story to fit in with their readers' millennial neuroses, and computer programmers in need of a few extra bob. Everyone gained, apart from the people who ended up paying for it all: i.e. you and me the taxpayers.

Yet at the time, the threat seemed so real. As bird flu did in 2006. And as global warming and rising sea levels still do today. There's a lesson in there, somewhere.

Misery Memoirs (see also Victim)

Ah, to be sure life was tough growing up in Killblarney. Every day, before dawn, Mam would beat the twelve of us with a shit-covered stick – 'If Oi've told ye once Oi've told ye a thousand times. Oi think it's disgusting the way ye let that syphilitic Uncle Craic-Head and his gang from the Killblarney Child Abuse Association have his way wid ye all, every night from dusk till dawn,' she'd say – before sending us, barefoot, on the 200-mile round trip to Dublin, on roads covered with broken glass, to buy fresh scorpions from the zoo so that when Da got back drunk from the pub, we'd all have them tied on to the whip he called 'the Lasher', ready for us to be flayed to within an inch of our lives – those of us who hadn't been killed earlier that afternoon by Father MacGinnis at the Christian Brothers Torture Academy. Little did I know how much worse things would get when I was adopted by a Californian family, the Felchers. They didn't call me by my name any more. They called me Poo. That's because that's all they ever fed me – poo, poo and more poo and no matter how hungry you were there was never enough because the cockroaches would always get there first, millions of them, you'd be fighting running battles with them to get to that dog bowl, which wasn't easy with your drunken step-mom pouring bottles of bleach on your skin to make you go white – because I had black skin as well, you see – and it was at times like this I could never forget what my grandmother went through at Auschwitz; which I'll be saving for volume three of my bestselling series *I'm Not Making It Up, It Really Happened And Any Of My Relatives Who Says I'm Making It Up Is A Damned Fool Because If They Play Along With It They Could Get A Few Bestsellers Out Of This One, Too.*

Monbiot, George

Posho green activist (see also Porritt, Jonathon; Goldsmith, Zac) who, despite having enjoyed all the fruits of the capitalist system and English tradition in the neoclassical surrounds of Stowe public school, now wants to: ban hunting; replace capitalism with the barter system; force everyone to travel to work by coracle, unicycle or Shanks's pony; make juggling compulsory; require all clothes to be fashioned from scratchy, undyed, renewable organically grown hemp and make us all live in caves or yurts –

each with a windmill. Also claims that global warming (*qv*) denial is as bad as Holocaust denial.

Possibly needs to study history more closely – and lighten up a bit.

Moore, Michael

Lardy propagandist and 'Ordinary Joe' plutocrat; unwitting election agent for George W. Bush. Decent Americans so loathed the shrill lefty triumphalism of *Bowling For Columbine* and *Fahrenheit 9/11* that they just couldn't bear to vote for any presidential candidate of whom Moore might approve.

Multiculturalism

Whoever thought up the name multiculturalism was an evil genius. Short of 'serendipity' or 'incredibleorgasm' or, maybe, 'topnotch-blowjob', you'd be really quite hard pushed to find a word so heartily guaranteed to win widespread and unquestioning popular support.

Multiculturalism. Mmm. Nice. So that must mean: ebony – and all the other races, creeds and cultures – and ivory living together in perfect harmony; fresh food from around the globe in our shops, markets and restaurants; music from drum 'n' bass to dub; doing really well at the cricket, thanks to our Sikh spin-bowling secret weapon; top-quality imported Jamaican weed; and so on.

If that's what multiculturalism really meant – and you'd be amazed how many people still think it does – few of us would have much cause for complaint. But it doesn't mean that and it never did. Multiculturalism is a very specific political philosophy which, instead of bringing different cultures and races together in one big happy melting pot (*qv*) has as its aim the exact opposite: to emphasise people's differences.

Now just how stupid and destructive an idea is that? You have waves and waves of immigrants coming to Britain because they like what the place stands for and because presumably it's nicer than wherever they've come from. But then, instead of giving them the tools to get on and improve their lot by encouraging them to integrate with their host society, you say: 'Don't try to be British. Try to fit in as little as possible. You may earn less money and your children may be more miserable and society will be more fragmented and racism will increase – but at least you'll retain your cultural pride.'

Apart from a few staunch old lefties like Ken Livingstone (*qv*), pretty much everyone realises what a disaster multiculturalism has been – even including the current chairman of the Commission for Racial Equality.

The problem is that it's the few staunch old lefties who are now running our charities, advisory bodies, schools, universities, government departments, local councils and public services. When, for example, an application was made to the Heritage Lottery Fund for a grant to help preserve for the nation an extremely rare fourteenth-century illuminated prayer book called the *Macclesfield Psalter*, it met with little sympathy. 'And how,' the grants officer wanted to know, 'would this be relevant to the owner of the local Chinese takeaway?'

Mutilated Body

Six prison officers were awarded damages in excess of £1 million in 2006 after witnessing 'a scene of gothic horror' when one prisoner killed and mutilated another – removing his liver, spleen and one eye and announcing: 'I was just about to eat his heart.' This was hardcore – much juicier than anything we got to see in *The Silence Of The Lambs* or even *The Texas Chainsaw Massacre*. But worth up to £200,000 a head in damages? I'm not so sure.

When you have chosen a job which entails working with violent criminals and potential psychos cooped up in tiny cells and not given enough exercise, don't riots, slicings, beatings and so on rather go with the territory? And isn't it a prison officer's job to get there before an inmate gets strangled and cut to pieces, not after?

Myanmar (see also Beijing)

A good name for a cat that mewls a lot, maybe. But not for a proper country. Burma is miles better. And a Burmese actually is a cat.

Nature vs Nurture

Next time you find yourself queuing for the security checks at the airport during the school holidays have a look at the little girls. Every one of them will be carrying almost identical pieces of baggage: in one hand, a dolly, in the other, a pink trolley-case containing all dolly's clothes. Now consider this: do any of them look like future adults whose lives are going to be blighted if phallocentric society manages to deny them a career as plumbers, car mechanics or quantum physicists?

Girls and boys are different. For almost anyone who has ever had children, it's mind-blowingly, gobsmackingly obvious right from the off – long, long before any form of pernicious, sexist social conditioning could reasonably be blamed for having influenced their behaviour. So why, pray, do we still allow feminists, lefties and government policy makers to bully us into pretending otherwise?

In the seventies – the era when some right-on parents actually believed they could change the world by denying their sons guns and their daughters dolls – they did at least have the excuse of ignorance. Today, though, thanks to the research into autism (or 'extreme male-brain syndrome') done by Simon Baron-Cohen at Cambridge University, we now have scientific proof of what commonsense has told us all along: that there are fundamental differences between the average male brain and the average female brain.

Girlie-type brains, Baron-Cohen tells us, are geared towards 'empathising', while boy-type ones are geared towards 'systematising'. This doesn't mean you can't be a girl with a boy-type brain or a boy with a girl-type brain. It just means that there's a damned good biological reason why more girls tend to end up doing caring, social-skill jobs like nursing and speech therapy; and why more boys tend to end up as surgeons and engineers. And an even better one why the government and organisations like the Equal Opportunities Commission ought not to be squandering millions every year trying to force humankind to act in defiance of nature.

NHS

Whenever anyone in Britain has the temerity to criticise the National Health Service you always get follow-up letters in the newspaper from people who've recently had hospital treatment and want to say just how MARVELLOUS the doctors and nurses were, and how FIRST CLASS the medical care. Well what were they expecting? Gruel, torture and conditions modelled on the punishment block of the nastiest prison in Equatorial Guinea?

The traditional function of nurses and doctors is to care for the sick. The sort of person these professions attract tends, ergo, to be a reasonably caring type – someone who sees their mission in life to comfort the distressed, alleviate pain and treat illness wheresoever they find it. What these professions don't tend to attract is the sort of person who might go: 'Urrghh. Look at all the hideous pustules on your body! I'm not treating you, ugly boy!' Or: ' 'ey! 'ey! Guess what? You're gonna love this! You've only got three months to live.' So really, no matter how caring and dedicated most of the doctors and nurses working within the NHS may be, the fact that they are that way hardly constitutes an argument.

Such, though, is the rose-tinted idiocy that tends to inform all public debate on the National Health Service. The NHS's waiting lists for elective major surgery are getting longer, its hospitals grow shabbier, its debts are mounting and its wards are so riddled with MRSA you'd probably stand a better chance of survival operating on yourself at home with a rusty bread knife than risking any form of in-patient surgery. Yet still we go on deluding ourselves that our National Health Service is the 'envy of the world'.

Envy of the Third World maybe. That would explain some of the 100,000 health tourists who flock to Britain every year to sponge off our system, lengthen our wait for treatment and cost UK taxpayers somewhere between £200 million and £2 billion.

Doctors do pretty well out of it, too. The NHS wastes an estimated £100 million every year paying GP practices for patients they don't even have: these are the 3.5 million ghost patients who, despite having died or moved out of the area have remained on GPs' lists. In 2006, the average GP was earning over £100,000 each year – double the figure of 2000.

Then there are the hospital consultants who, in 2004 alone, snaffled from the NHS a tidy £85 million in fees. And the growing band of backroom administrators who, every year since the mid-nineties, have been adding to the NHS's wage costs by £1.5 billion. And let's not even begin to think about the £2 million the NHS spends every year to give computer training to its porters and cleaners. Or the £100,000 it spent on leaflets warning people to stay out of the sun.

The NHS is a behemoth out of control. It is the world's third largest employer after the Chinese army and the Indian State Railway, and growing bigger and more expensive all the time, with no appreciable improvement in the quality of the service it is offering the taxpayer. According to a 2004 report commissioned by the Office for National Statistics, the NHS may be wasting about £6 billion a year as rising inefficiency reduces its productivity.

Why is nothing being done to address this scandal? Because there is no political mileage in doing so. So pervasive is our sentimentality (see Cameron, Dave) about the NHS that we refuse to submit the organisation to any form of rational analysis. Since 1948 when the NHS was established a great many other aspects of our lives have improved: restaurant cuisine no longer consists of brown Windsor soup made with water and gravy powder; flying abroad is cheaper than chips; you don't have to wait two months before your telephone is installed. Yet within the NHS the grim spirit of post-war Britain lingers on: it continues to treat us, not like discerning consumers who deserve something in return for what we've paid for – but like craven supplicants who should jolly well be grateful for whatever half-baked service we get.

Nigger

The name of Guy Gibson's dog, which puts broadcasters in a dreadful quandary every time they show *The Dambusters*. Do they bleep it out and sacrifice the 1954 film classic's artistic integrity and historical accuracy to the dark forces of PC? Or do they keep the name intact and upset commentators like David Aaronovitch (*qv*), who argues that it gives 'huge and unnecessary offence to millions of fellow citizens'?

Nitty Gritty

When at a 2002 Police Federation conference Minister of State at the Home Office John Denham suggested it was time to, 'get down to the nitty gritty' he was warned by one police constable, Chris Jefford, head of the Met's training directorate, that this phrase was politically unacceptable and could earn a disciplinary charge for racism.

How so? Because, constable Jefford explained, the phrase was thought to refer to slaves on the lowest decks of slave ships.

Yet the first recorded use of the phrase was in 1954. 'It is inconceivable,' says internet lexicographer Michael Quinion, 'that it should have been around since the slave-ship days without someone writing it down.'

Still on the police banned list, though – obviously.

Non-Competitive Sports Days

Life's a bastard and we're all going to die. But while we're alive we're going to have to fight to survive: fight for our jobs; fight to get enough sex; fight for a seat on the easyJet flight next to the person we're travelling with rather than the chav we spotted drinking in the bar at 6.30 this morning and thought, 'Oh, God, please not him.' Because that's the kind of world we live in: an evil, bastard, dog-eat-dog, shark-swallows-minnow and whale-eats-plankton, survival-of-the-fittest competitive one.

Now, clearly, the sooner your children learn this the better. That way they'll have an instant advantage over all their peers whose parents weren't as far-sighted and quick-thinking as you – the loser brats, known as the competition. Not only will this give your children a vital head start in the great race of life; but also, more importantly, it will benefit you. On the macro scale it will marginally increase your chances of being able to watch your child win the Formula One championship or Wimbledon or the Most Stupidly Rich Hedge Fund Manager With The Biggest Private Caribbean Island Of The Year Award. On the micro scale, it ought to ensure that the fruit of your loins doesn't humiliate you too badly at the school sports day.

But hey, wait a minute: what's that you heard your child's primary school head teacher (he's a man so really he's a headmaster, but that's not a term he understands) just say? 'We're not doing competitive sports this year.' Surely not. A non-competitive sports day? Isn't that a bit like having a food-free meal? A liquid-free drink? A death-free war? A pleasure-free wank? Why, the man is having us on, he must be. No way would any of us here have taken a valuable afternoon out of the office in order to stand kicking our heels while our children mill around a field doing bugger all. We can do that every weekend in the playground.

Tragically, though, the head teacher was not joking. It seems that he has got hold of one of the Primary Sports Day Toolkits provided by a body called Sport England which, with hearty government endorsement, show schools how to run their sports days with all the nasty competitive element removed. 'The trouble with traditional sports days is that too many youngsters are left out as spectators,' Sport England's chief explains. But thanks to this toolkit there are fun opportunities aplenty for everyone, no matter how pathetically malco or crap (though these aren't quite the terms the document employs). Among the twenty-eight problem-solving games on offer are 'bean-bag pick up' and 'stranded-sheep', all carefully designed so that 'pupils of lower ability are not exposed'.

There's just one small problem: the kids hate it. In fact, they're even more mightily pissed off about this PC charade than their parents are. Why? Because even the feeblest and most avowedly unsporty among them recognises that this is not a natural state of affairs, that a game you can't win is no game at all, that your whole raison d'être when you're a kid at school is to find some way of proving yourself better than all the others.

Some kids compete by being first to get the coolest toys, some by being more disgusting, more daring, more clown-like, better at spelling, better-read, better at football, better at climbing high ropes. So when you remove the competitive element from school sports days, you're not suddenly creating an ideal world where all children are equal and none suffers from low self-esteem. All you're doing is penalising the athletic ones – the ones who quite possibly don't have many other talents apart from being able to run fast or jump high. For these kids sports day is the one moment in their year when they can really shine. And now, in the name of fairness, schools all over Britain are denying them that opportunity. Is it any wonder we make such a poor showing in the Olympics these days?

NSPCC

Abused any kids recently? You haven't? What kind of weirdo are you? Of course, you abuse kids. We all abuse kids. Even if you're not guilty of full-on sexual abuse – which happens a lot more than you think, you know (in your house especially, probably) – there are lots of other kinds of abuse, very nearly as bad.

Ever smacked your kids, for example? Well, that's abuse. That's violence against children that is; that's physical assault in fact, which is why we at the NSPCC have been lobbying the government to have it banned. Think it's none of our business, do you? Think how you discipline your children is nothing to do with the government, let alone a charity with no democratic mandate? Well, for a start, that's a sign that you've got something to hide because if you didn't you wouldn't be so defensive would you? And it also goes to show how little you know about the cycle of violence, because what you're doing when you clip your child round the ear – exposing them, we might point out, to the very real possibility of brain damage — is teaching them that violence is an appropriate response to inappropriate behaviour and it never is, got that? Never. NEVER. VIOLENCE IN ANY SHAPE OR FORM, BUT ESPECIALLY IF IT'S SMACK-SHAPED AND AGAINST CHILDREN IS ALWAYS WRONG.

Oh, and if you've never smacked a child, that doesn't let you off the hook either because our mission at the NSPCC is to create a society where children are 'loved, respected and valued', and I'll bet you haven't always done that have you? Bet when you've had a football booted through your front window, or they've dragged a key playfully down the side of your car, or they've run screaming round the pub while you were trying to have a quiet drink, or they've let their pit bull terrier swallow your cat; I'll bet you weren't willing to understand their needs and appreciate that what they most need is love and tolerance, not condemnation (see also Cameron, Dave).

So you see the problem with child abuse in Britain isn't just other people's problem, it's everyone's problem. And most especially it's your problem, which is why we intend to shove our campaign leaflets through your letter box whether you like it or not (and if you think it's junk mail, well then only an abuser would think something as pure and wholesome as an NSPCC charity leaflet was junk mail). And it's why we're going to put up posters and run expensive TV ads (did you know, in 1992 we spent £24 million campaigning on public education?) designed to jerk you out of your smug, middle-class complacency by implying that it's you, yes you, smug middle-class types who are responsible for the majority of child abuse in this country, not itinerant step-dads on housing estates, whatever the evidence might suggest.

The public's right behind us, too. In our last survey we asked: 'Do you think it's right that children should have heated pencils driven into their eyes by smug middle-class parents?' To which no fewer than 99.1 per cent of respondents said 'No'.

Hmm. And the NSPCC wonders why some of us don't want to give them our money.

Nuclear Power

Atomkraft? Nein Danke! That's what the stickers on the back windows of clapped-out VW Combis always used to say in the seventies and the eighties – Nuclear Power? No Thanks! – and that's where the green lobby is still stuck. They don't want to talk about it and they don't want to think about it. Nuclear power is bad, nyah nyah nyah go away, not listening, don't care what you say, talk to the hand.

If they paused to analyse the issue – as the renowned environmentalist James Lovelock, inventor of the Gaia hypothesis has done – they might realise that nuclear power is the answer to their prayers: a clean, cheap, safe – yes SAFE! and efficient form of power which can supply all Britain's energy needs while emitting hardly any greenhouse gases.

But saying 'no to nuclear' has never been about reasoned argument. It's about gut politics, primitive superstition and scientific ignorance, as in: nuclear power is associated with atom bombs and Hiroshima and Cold War terror, and it's made by scary scientists in the pay of big government and faceless corporations, ergo it must be bad.

Among the few environmentalists talking sense in the debate is the Liberal peer Lord Taverne, who believes our terror of nuclear power stems largely from a misunderstanding about the dangers of radiation.

He points out, for example, that after the atom bombing of Hiroshima and Nagasaki, thousands died in the immediate blast, and thousands more as a result of burns afterwards. But the prediction that the radiation would lead to terrible after-effects on those who did survive and on their (then unborn) children was proved quite wrong (see also Chernobyl). In fact, studies found, their life expectancy had actually *increased*.

Low doses of radiation – even ones up to 100 times higher than the 1 millisievert (msv) per year current health and safety standards allow us to be exposed to – actually have a beneficial effect on human health, including on some forms of cancer. The death rate from leukaemia among nuclear industry workers in Canada, for example, is 68 per cent below the national average.

Perhaps if facts like this were more widely known, the British public would be a little less resistant to the idea of nuclear power. Such information might make us reflect on the fact that, whatever green scaremongers tell us, nuclear energy will do infinitely less damage to our environment than wind turbines (*qv*) will. It might also provide our only hope of not being held economic hostage by the French.

While we dither and agonise over nuclear energy, you see, the French are building nuclear power stations like mad. Imagine the horror if, in thirty years' time we had to go cap-in-hand to France every time we needed to supplement what risible amount of energy we'd managed to squeeze from our crappy wind turbines. The agony! The humiliation! The expense! The horror!

Oil, It's All About

What does your car run on: wind? Lucozade? *Guardian* editorials? The one I drive runs on petrol. As indeed does the national and global economy. Which is why I find it hard to get too exercised when I hear the phrase, 'it's all about oil' being used to criticise Western intervention in the Middle East.

It's all about oil. And your problem with that would be . . . ?

Organic

Look, don't get me wrong, I'm as gullible as the next idiot. I'll invariably pay the extra in Sainsbury's for the organic carrots; I'll look at 'prime rib of organic Highland beef' on the menu and suddenly not begrudge the fact that it's going to cost me half a year's wages; I'd rather feed my children on organic than non-organic; when the new potatoes taste of new potatoes and my dinner hostess tells me they're from her weekly organic delivery box I'll go: 'Gosh, you really notice the difference with organic, don't you?' But I only do all this because I'm stupid and lazy and easily led.

Organic is one of the great con tricks of the age, a way of persuading well-meaning, middle-class families to pay 40 per cent over the odds for their pongy meat and stunted, blighted, misshapen vegetables under the sad delusion that they will somehow make them better and healthier and happier.

But if organic food's so good for the environment how come over 70 per cent of the stuff we consume in Britain has to be imported? If it's so natural, how come it's allowed to be sprayed with inorganic copper sulphate – which is known to kill more insects and be less effective than many more modern types of fungicide? And if it tastes so much better – how do you explain the cotton-wool-flavoured organically grown Dutch beef tomato?

'At least it doesn't give you cancer,' you'll say. But nor does non-organic food. This notion that any foodstuff not approved by the Soil Association must be, perforce, laced with noxious chemicals, deadly carcinogens and vicious pesticide residues is just another urban myth put about by green fundamentalists. As Sir John Krebs, when he was chairman of the Food Standards Agency, once put it in *Nature*: 'A single cup of coffee contains natural carcinogens equal to at least a year's worth of carcinogenic synthetic residues in the diet.'

Sure, not everything farmers spray on their fields is delicious and wholesome. But then, everything we eat and drink, organic or no, contains deadly poisons of one kind or another. According to Dick Taverne in *The March Of Unreason* there is evidence to suggest that people exposed to higher than normal levels of pesticides – farmers, millers, foresters – actually have much lower levels of cancer overall. This phenomenon of low-dose beneficial effects, known as hormesis, also applies to another of the green lobby's pet hates: radiation (see also Nuclear Power; Chernobyl).

All right then. But surely if the punters want to go on buying organic food and farmers want to go on growing it, it's hardly going to do any harm, is it? Not so. Organic farming is, by its nature, less efficient than non-organic farming and therefore requires more land (which might otherwise be set aside to encourage greater biodiversity); therefore organic food costs more to produce and thus to buy (putting it further out of reach of the poor). As the Indian biotechnologist C. S. Prakash has said: 'The only thing sustainable about organic farming in the developing world is that it sustains poverty and malnutrition.'

Paedophilia

The world's worst crime.

Partner, when used in the context of marriage/ sexual relationship rather than business

An infallible sign that the person using this term won't be any fun at your dinner party.

Passenger Profiling

'Hmm. Now which of these is most likely to blow us all up?' you wonder, casting an anxious, sidelong glance at your fellow passengers waiting to board flight 013 to New York. The elderly Irish nun, perhaps, with the walking stick? Or the fifty-something banker and his blonde trophy wife heading off for their fifth-anniversary shopping spree? Or the white, middle-class family of four chattering excitedly about the galleries and Central Park and the view from the Empire State building? Or the five young Middle-Eastern gentlemen with the shaven body hair and sweaty foreheads who seem to be travelling separately, yet will insist on exchanging knowing glances, while worrying perpetually at their prayer beads and murmuring to themselves what sounds like – if your schoolboy Arabic serves you correctly – 'These infidel dogs must die!'

'Nope,' you think to yourself. 'There's really no way anyone could ever guess. No wonder most airlines are so reluctant to introduce passenger profiling! It's racist, it's discriminatory and it might give people the wholly unfounded impression that young Muslim males present a significantly greater terrorist risk than any other section of society.'

If this is how you feel about 'passenger profiling', don't worry, you're in excellent company. Metropolitan Police Chief Super-intendent Ali Dizaei says that security checks based on religion or ethnicity will create a new offence of 'travelling whilst Asian', adding: 'I don't think there's a stereotypical image of a terrorist.' Tory shadow minister Oliver Letwin appeared to agree when in 2001, shortly after 9/11, he declared: 'I wouldn't like to see groups of people segregated as one goes through the departure lounge because they happen to come from whatever is that month's risk category – being deeply frisked in the way everyone else isn't.'

Well Ali and Olly, of course we respect the sincerity and generosity of your position but, unfortunately, the rest of us can't quite live up to your high moral standards. What with the way things are going, we've been getting a bit squeamish about flying recently. We've got this terrible hang up – call it cowardice if you will – about catching a plane and being blown to smithereens before we get to where we're going. In fact, we're so worried about it we simply don't give a toss any more about all those PC pieties we could just about tolerate in the days before 9/11 when there wasn't quite so much at stake. Given the choice between offending a few minorities and staying alive, well, sorry, but it's a no-brainer.

Passionate

'We're as passionate about business as we are about pleasure,' says a propaganda website for North East England. 'Passionate about parks,' declares South Tyneside local authority. 'I'm passionate about change in public services,' announces Tony Blair.

Bollocks you are. It's bad enough having to be reminded every time you go to the cinema that your local fleapit is 'Passionate about film' (that's a relief then – and there we all were quaking in the stalls at the thought that they might be only 'mildly interested in film,' or 'definitely not averse to film,' or 'up for a film so long as there's nothing better on, like maybe indoor bowls or the snooker') but to hear the word being adopted by local authorities and politicians really is a semiological abuse too far.

Apart from the utter fraudulence of it all (passionate about your wife, your children, your favourite rock band, maybe; but passionate about 'change in public services'? Puh-lease), what sticks in the craw is the assumption that we're all so deeply immersed in the warm, slushy pool of post-Diana touchy-feeliness that passion trumps everything – intelligence, logic, reason, commonsense, practicality, the lot.

Well I'm sorry, but if you had to make a list of ideal qualities in our governing classes, passion would come somewhere between 'willingness to take a bribe' and 'preparedness to sell our country's interests down the river at every opportunity'. Passion is a nice thing for me to feel about stamp collecting and you to feel about Chelsea Football Club. But when it comes to members of the government making important decisions, passionate is the opposite of what we need. Politics may be about passion. Government should be about reason.

Passive Smoking

'The effects of other people smoking in my presence is so small it doesn't worry me.' Sir Richard Doll, discoverer of the link between smoking and cancer, on Desert Island Discs.

Passive smoking does not exist – at least not in the sense in which it is used by anti-smoking campaigners. Spend a day, a night, a whole year working in a smoky bar and you are not suddenly going to drop dead of a heart attack or keel over with lung cancer. You just won't, seriously. It's a complete and utter myth.

How do we know this? Between 1959 and 1989, two American researchers named James Enstrom and Geoffrey Kabat conducted the world's only major long-term investigation into the subject, surveying no fewer than 118,094 Californians. Fierce anti-smoking campaigners themselves, they began the research because they wanted to prove once and for all what a pernicious, socially damaging habit smoking was. Their research was initiated by the American Cancer Society and supported by the anti-smoking Tobacco Related Disease Research Program.

At least it was at first. But then something rather embarrassing happened. Much to their surprise, Kabat and Enstrom discovered that exposure to environmental tobacco smoke (i.e. passive smoking), no matter how intense or prolonged, creates no significantly increased risk of heart disease or lung cancer.

From being the heroes of the health lobby, Enstrom and Kabat became its number one villains. The American Cancer Society and the Tobacco Related Disease Research Program dropped them like a hot potato, and the only way Enstrom and Kabat could afford to complete their research was with the backing of their former arch enemies – the cigarette industry.

The moral of the story, unfortunately, is not that truth will prevail but rather that truth will be mercilessly squashed if it's the wrong sort of truth. Enstrom and Kabat – honest, diligent researchers whose only concern has been the advance of scientific knowledge – have had their integrity smeared and their research either damned or buried by what they call 'enforcers of political correctness who pose as disinterested scientists but are willing to use base means to trash a study whose results they dislike'. It was because of the passive smoking risk that the government felt able to justify its draconian ban on smoking in all public places. Thus has another liberty been stolen from us on the basis of a total lie.

PC PCs (see also Nitty Gritty)

In 2006 a nineteen-year-old female candidate for a job in the police service passed all her written tests only to be rejected at the interview stage for failing to show sufficient 'diversity (*qv*) awareness'. Asked what she would do if she needed advice, she had made the mistake of answering: 'I would go to my sergeant and ask him for help.' By referring to the sergeant as 'him', she had revealed her lack of understanding of gender issues.

And we wonder why the police are so useless when our homes get burgled.

People For The Ethical Treatment Of Animals (PETA)

People? Hey, we like them – people are nice. Ethical? That's good too: noble, lofty, considered and considerate. Animals? Love 'em, can't get enough of 'em. For? The? Treatment? Of? Nothing wrong with them either. So that must mean that PETA is just the kind of life-enhancing charity we should be joining and giving all our money to, right?

Er, no. It's bad enough that they try to bribe our innocent, sausage-loving kids with iPod nanos to 'Go Veggie'. But what they also want to do is: stop us watching lions, tigers, elephants or even horses at the circus; stop the bull running at Pamplona; stop us wearing fur and stop our guardsmen outside Buckingham Palace wearing bearskins (they want them to use synthi-skins instead, which PETA claims work just as well – but they don't, the army tried them and they go all manky when it rains).

Sure, PETA's membership abounds with supermodels and babes because that's what a lot of pretty girls in their teens and twenties are looking for – they need a cause, and the cuter and furrier it is the better. But come motherhood and winter they start to see sense. Kids do love a bacon sandwich, see. And a sable coat is just so snuggly when the temperature has dropped below freezing. Or when your latest modelling contract pays you a fat fortune to wear one.

Pharmacists

In France you can go into any chemist's with a mushrooom and they'll tell you expertly whether it's something totally deadly, like, perhaps a destroying angel, or completely delicious like a cep or a parasol mushroom. Thanks to material obtained by the *Times Educational Supplement* under the Freedom of Information Act we now know that the pass mark for students on the pharmacy course at De Montfort University, Leicester has in recent years been as low as 26 per cent. Doesn't that suddenly make you exceedingly grateful that all most British chemists do is dispense condoms and aspirin?

Polar Bears Killed By Global Warming

We've all read the stories: ice melting earlier in summer and freezing later in winter means polar bears have less time to hunt for seals on the ice floes and are either starving to death or swimming too far out to sea and drowning. 'Right, that's bloody it, I've had enough,' we've all shrieked into our cornflakes. 'I can just about cope with Kilimanjaro (qv) losing its pretty white top and I suppose, if I'm honest, I couldn't care that much whether or not Tuvalu sinks beneath the waves. But polar bears?!!! They're so white and fluffy (see also Baby Seals) and loveable that under no circumstances must any more of them be allowed to die. Not even if it means no one ever taking a foreign holiday again. Not even if it means banning all cars. Not even if every single one of us has to commit suicide, because it is our fault after all, we deserve it, whereas polar bears they're pure and innocent and perfect.'

Luckily, though, it's not as bad as you think. It turns out, once you examine the data, that polar bears aren't in danger from global warming at all. Yes, it's true that there are parts of the world where polar bear populations are declining, but there are other areas of the world where they're actually increasing. But here's the funny bit – the one they don't mention in all those scaremongering reports by the World Wildlife Fund (WWF) and Greenpeace: it's the areas which are getting colder (notably in Baffin Bay, between North America and Greenland) where the polar bear population is in decline; in areas where it's getting warmer (notably in the Pacific region between Siberia and Alaska), the polar bear population is increasing. It's the exact opposite, in other words, of what the eco-doom merchants have been telling us.

Poles, The

There's nothing bad you can say about the Poles. Heroic, doomed cavalry charges against German tanks; ace fighter pilots; great builders too – and miles cheaper than all those English cowboys who got driven out of the market once the Polish invasion began and every second high-street shop started selling large jars of pickled white cabbage. They won't stay, of course, because they think Britain's a dump. Which is quite damning, really, coming from people who only recently escaped half a century under Nazism and Communism.

Polytechnics

In the old days, the local poly was where you ended up if you weren't quite clever enough to get into university. The college building would be a decaying sixties box made of concrete, chipboard and asbestos and the teachers would be chippy second-raters in donkey jackets. But at least being at poly somewhere grimly urban like Leeds or Luton earned you a street cred your posho university mates could only dream of, plus you got to see The Smiths before anyone else had heard of them. Then at the end you'd come out with a vocational qualification called a higher national diploma (HND) which, though not a degree, was just the thing if you had ambitions to become a road-surface-debris remover or a waste disposal technician.

But then in the eighties, Margaret Thatcher had the bright idea of letting all the polytechnics upgrade themselves to universities. The teaching quality and admissions standards remained just as dismal, but now these once-sneered-at establishments could dignify themselves with poncy names like Greater Northern University (formerly Grimthorpe Poly) and award actual, proper degrees, not dissimilar in value to the ones you can buy on American websites for a few dollars a throw.

Has the elevation of our polys resulted in a dramatic increase in the nation's cleverness? Unfortunately not. Rather, it has flooded the market with delusional morons who imagine that because they have a degree in windsurfing, graphic novel studies and vineyard management from the University of Greater England, they're somehow entitled to a job.

Porritt, Jonathon

Posho green activist (see also Goldsmith, Zac) with major social advantage over George Monbiot (*qv*): he went to Eton, not Stowe.

Poverty

Formerly: a state of extreme indigence.
Now: able to afford Sky, but only the basic package, not Sky Sports.

Until at least the mid-twentieth century, poverty meant being really poor. You were thin and malnourished because of your meagre diet; you dressed in rags; you lived in an unheated rat-infested hovel; you perished movingly in novels by Charles Dickens. And you couldn't afford the basket of basic foodstuffs (cheese, porridge, bread) devised in 1901 by the social reformer Seebohm Rowntree as a benchmark to define poverty.

You could afford them now, though. In fact, even if you have central heating; a fridge; a cooker; a TV; a DVD player; a satellite dish; free medicine and a massive whale-like belly not necessarily indicative of imminent death by starvation, you can still – according to the most popular definition used by social scientists, Labour politicians, and Polly Toynbee – be 'living in poverty'.

To qualify, all you need to do is be earning/scrounging less than 60 per cent of the median national wage. By this definition, if Bill Gates moved to Britain and brought all his money with him, poverty would immediately increase. Also, no matter how rich we got, even if every single one of us had a Porsche, a swimming pool, and a house on an island in Dubai, there would still be a percentage of us 'living in poverty'. But not, perhaps, as someone living in a mud hut in the Sudan would understand it.

Prejudice (see also Discrimination)

Without prejudice we would all be in deepest do-do. Thanks to prejudice, we know that when a white van driver carves you up it's not a good idea to flick him the V sign; that you don't go into a pub full of drunken, post-match Millwall fans wearing the colours of the team that's just beaten them three–nil; that when you see a gang of teenagers in hoodies coming up the street towards you at 3 a.m. on a Saturday, you make yourself scarce.

Everyone is prejudiced for prejudice is a function of being alive and continuing to stay alive. You observe the world, you form judgements based on your previous experience and you apply them to all future experiences until proven otherwise.

In recent times, the race relations industry has very successfully hijacked the word to mean a form of thought-crime of which only people of Anglo-Saxon origin (the Scots, the Irish and the Welsh are exempt) can ever be guilty. This is very prejudiced of it.

Prescott, John

Because of his chucklesome looks (Les Dawson, with menace), delusions of grandeur (asked once who should play him in a movie, he plumped for Marlon Brando in *On The Waterfront*), his way with words ('The green belt is a Labour policy and we intend to build on it') and, of course, the jocular nickname ('Two Jags'; later 'Two Shags'), John Prescott has sometimes been mistaken for a semi-loveable comedy figure.

Really, though, if his life was a film it would be called *Circus Of Blood* and he'd be the one playing Evil Clown whose smiling face hides tears, bitterness and simmering psychotic rage. One by one he would butcher his colleagues – the Bulgarian strong man; the Russian acrobats; the twirly moustached ringmaster and, yes, even nice sweet Pony Girl, who was the only person who was ever kind to him when she found him once sobbing, alone in the elephant enclosure.

All his political ideas were bad. All his schemes were wrong.

John Prescott was never funny. He was absolutely bloody terrifying.

Pressure Groups, Single Issue

A child has been killed in a tragic, apple-falling-on-head incident. 'Accidents like this are extremely unusual,' admits a policeman in the newspaper report. 'In fact I can't recall one like it in my twenty-five years of service.' Maybe so, but that doesn't stop a single-issue pressure group, Mothers Against Apple Danger, being given voluminous space at the end of the report to demand further action.

'This is exactly the kind of apple-related danger we've been warning about all along,' says MAAD's spokeswoman Valerie Nuthead, who slipped on a rotten apple once and is out for revenge. 'Britain's orchards are an accident waiting to happen, and unless further action is taken we estimate that up to a million children every year will remain under threat of death or injury.

'MAAD demands a sweeping programme of apple-related

safety measures, including health and safety training for every apple grower; the licensing of all orchards; a minimum age limit for apple pickers; compulsory warning signs; tall apple trees and heavier varieties of apple to be phased out by 2012; larger windbreaks to be installed round all orchards so as to reduce the risk of accidental apple-falling; orchards to be designated hard-hat areas; a national education programme to advocate the merits of softer, lighter plums over hard, aggressive apples; all apples to be phased out completely by 2050.'

Asked to comment on MAAD's proposals, a government minister says: 'Apple-related injuries are something this government takes very seriously and we shall be inviting MAAD to form part of our new task force on fruit danger avoidance.'

And so it is that a single mad person with an axe to grind, a newspaper reporter keen to pad out his copy and a government department with a yen for publicity, can conspire in the creation of yet another oppressive, pointless, expensive law that sends the rest of us scratching our heads and wondering: 'What the hell was that one all about?'

This is how single-issue campaigns work. While they may sound very noble in theory – what price, after all, a child's life? – in practice, what they do is give a voice to tiny minorities of victims seeking to influence the majority with their own prejudices.

Consider the 1996 Dunblane massacre. If any of us had been unlucky enough to have our children shot dead in that kinder-garten class by the deranged Thomas Hamilton, we too would have campaigned as passionately and vociferously as the Snowdrop group did for the banning of all handguns in Britain. But would the government have been right to accede to our demands?

Hardly. If our laws were based on the views of victims' families, drink drivers would be crucified, rapists castrated, drugs dealers strung up and murderers lynched. But one of the benefits of living in a representative democracy is that we no longer have to submit ourselves to this type of gang rule. Now we elect governments capable of differentiating between the passionate demands of the few at any given moment and the broader, long-term interests of the many. At least that's the idea.

How has Britain benefited from the ban on handguns, introduced in 1997 by the government as a cheap popularity-winning measure after Dunblane? Yet another law-abiding minority – in this case target shooters and gun collectors – have been denied the chance to enjoy their hobby; our once medal-winning Olympic small arms team has been forced to train in Switzerland and has plunged down the international rankings; gun crime has more than doubled; the number of illegal handguns has soared.

And will another Dunblane be averted? Hardly. The next killer will just use a machete or a home-made bomb instead. That's the thing about insane mass-murderers: never ones to allow well-meaning single-issue pressure groups to get in the way of a killing spree.

Prison, Cost Of

Each prisoner costs you the taxpayer £37,000 per year. This seems quite a lot until you divide it by the number of us who pay tax – 31.5 million– and suddenly realise what an amazing bargain it is. It means you can nip down the corner shop for a pint of milk and a pack of Werther's Originals and still have enough change to keep around 17,021 thugs, rapists, joyriders, muggers and crazed psycho-killers safely behind bars for twelve whole months. Compare that with the amount you spend annually on, say, replacing at vast expense the electric windows on your car which have been smashed in by a passing thief and which you can't get back on the insurance because of your minimum excess charge. For about the same cost, you could imprison the entire car-theft population of Britain and throw away the key.

Private schools

What's so scary about private schools – particularly for those of us who can't afford them – is that pretty soon they will be the only places in Britain where a child can get a decent education.

Not decent as in 'complete with Olympic-size swimming pool, billion-pound arts-media-technology-and-hedge-fund-management centre, three-tennis-courts-per-child, plus daily aromatherapy massage and one-to-one happiness training sessions'. (Though you do seem to get all that, too, these days.) Just decent, as in 'a bit of grammar, a bit of Latin, at least one modern language, no swearing or ultra violence in class, homework expected to be done on time, Shakespeare plays read all the way through rather than "studied" in the form of microscopic textual gobbets sandwiched in an anthology between an extract from Maya Angelou (qv) and an anti-war poem by Benjamin Zephaniah'.

The standard excuse trotted out by Guardianistas is that, of course private schools do better because they can select their intake and their children come from comfortable, bookish back-grounds with pushy parents. But this is cant. Children from poor backgrounds can do just as well when given the opportunity, as the old grammar schools proved before Labour abolished them.

Why private schools really work is because that they can't afford not to. If a private school goes downhill, people stop sending their kids there, it loses its revenue and eventually it will close. There is such mechanism in the state system, which is far more concerned with the interests of teachers (especially lazy, useless ones, whom the teachers' unions have striven so successfully to render unsackable) and disruptive pupils (which schools are powerless to get rid of) than in those of parents or normal children.

It's no good blaming limited resources, either. As James Tooley, professor of education policy at Newcastle University has demonstrated, in India and Africa between 65 and 75 per cent of children in the poorest slums attend private schools (though not ones costing £26,000 a year, obviously; ones costing more like a few quid, but still a big chunk out of the parents' budget). Why? Because, as one father in a Kenyan slum put it, 'If you go to the market and are offered free fruit and vegetables, you know they'll be rotten. If you want fresh produce, you have to pay for it.'

Prohibition

Didn't work for booze, doesn't work for drugs. If I want to stick all my meagre earnings up my nose and acquire an attractive mono-nostril like soap star Daniella Westbrook, that's my prerogative. If, alternatively, I want to sit back and not take drugs while all my richer friends who do take them get poorer and unhappier then this, too, surely ought to be my right as a free citizen.

This isn't just a liberty issue either, it's a matter of solid pragmatism. Even if you're viscerally opposed to drugs (though God knows why: you do use alcohol and caffeine presumably?), you'll surely agree that it is a quite monstrous state of affairs the amount of our taxed income which goes on keeping dealers and drug users in prison, and paying policemen and customs officers to arrest them. And let's not forget the gun crime connected to the drugs industry. And all the burglaries and robberies committed by druggies to feed a habit which wouldn't be nearly so expensive if drugs were legalised.

'Yes, but what about the social consequences?' Oh, puh-lease. Do you honestly believe there's a single person out there who'd like to take drugs but isn't doing so because they're illegal? The country's awash with drugs. Even your nicely brought-up nephews and nieces are doing them. Legalising drugs wouldn't make the blindest bit of difference to the amount they consume; but it would mean a pastime, which most of the population have long since accepted as being as normal as drinking tea, would no longer lead to otherwise law-abiding lives being tarnished with a criminal record.

Queen, The

When we're about fourteen or fifteen some of us go through our angry anti-monarchical phase. 'Yeah, wot's she ever done to deserve all that wealth 'n' privilege? And why does she have to look so miserable all the time? And why can't she pay taxes like the rest of us? And why does she let her kids carry on the way they do? And why does she have to come over so aloof and remote? And why couldn't she be more like Princess Di? Come the revolution, she'll be the first against the wall!'

Saying this makes us feel very radical and insightful and mature. But then we grow up and realise: No, actually, she's wonderful.

She unites our nation in times of crisis. She binds us to our history and our traditions. She's a rock of stability and dignity in an age of fickleness and hysterical emotionalism. She helps us maintain a happy, mutually beneficial relationship with the countries of our former empire. She has sacrificed her personal life for a public one of neverending duty, responsibility and ordeal-by-ceremonial-native-dance. She stops us having to worry about boring constitutional matters because her role is so clearly defined, and nothing we ever try to replace her with is ever going to work nearly so well. She is the reason why we are never going to have a President Tony Blair.

Anyone with an ounce of sense and maturity knows all this to be true.

Those who don't are called republicans.

Reagan, Ronald

Ended the Cold War; transformed the US economy; brought peace, prosperity and stability to the world. The left – which still thinks of him as a dumb cowboy – will never forgive him for it.

Recycling (see also Anti-Racism; Diwali; Environment, The; Litter)

Principal topic at all state primary schools.

Right Wing (see also Left Wing)

Being right wing is synonymous with: crap taste in music; even worse taste in clothes; uselessness in bed; sexism; racism; a fondness for spanking, tarts dressed as French maids, water sports, and semi-auto-asphyxiation enjoyed while masturbating with an orange in your mouth; insider dealing; Nimbyism; wanton selfishness; environmental vandalism; philistinism; greed; stupidity; cruelty; mendacity; corruption; xenophobia; closed-mindedness; extremism; bigotry; adultery; and pure, unvarnished evil.

As a right winger myself, I can personally vouch that an awful lot of this is true – especially the bit about oranges. But what I don't quite understand is why it should be that right wingers should be seen to have the monopoly on nastiness and depravity.

Actually, that's a lie – I do understand. It's because, quite simply, the ideas of the liberal left are all so utterly impractical, stupid and wrong that none of them stands up to close intellectual scrutiny. Deep down, most lefties know this, which is why they have to find ways of winning the political argument without having to resort to tedious details like logic, truth or practicality. And what better way to close down the argument (*qv*) than by smearing the right-wing opposition as being such a bunch of complete wankers that nothing they say is of any value?

The evil genius behind this cunning strategy was an Italian Marxist called Antonio Gramsci (*qv*) who recognised that for the left to win the political war it must first win the cultural one. In other words, the left needed to infiltrate the university campuses, the arts and the media and create a cultural climate in which to be right wing was not merely a political affiliation but proof positive of moral deficiency.

Which, in short, is why today even right wingers think right wingers are tossers. It's not true though. Were the most prolific mass-murderers in history – Mao and Stalin – right wing? They were not. Nor, technically, was National Socialist Adolf Hitler. And Pol Pot wasn't exactly a card-carrying fascist either. So between them, evil lefties have killed millions more people than nice, cuddly right wingers ever did or will. Now can we stop hating ourselves, please?

Rock stars

'Rock stars. Is there anything they don't know?' asked Homer Simpson. They know, for example, that the only way of saving Africa is to pour billions more of your pounds into shoring up corrupt regimes, encouraging them to default on loans and providing barmy kleptocrats with ever larger fleets of Mercedes (see also Drop The Debt; Live Aid).

How do they know all this? Simple. Instead of filling their heads at school with nonsense like facts, they spent their time singing, strumming their guitars and having a lot more sex than you ever will. Then they strummed a bit more. Had more sex. Took drugs. Got a record deal. This led to more sex, drugs and strumming. Then they had a hit record and got famous, enabling them to enjoy truly stupendous quantities of sex and drugs while travelling around in jets and limos and staying in expensive hotels. Which in turn gave them access to prime ministers, popes and presidents who hang on their every word. Oh, and somewhere along the way, they became instant experts on how to make the world perfect.

Roll out

Does it mean, 'start with immediate effect'? 'Put into preparation'? 'Introduce gradually'? Or, 'consider as one of a raft of proposals'?

No one has ever worked this one out and no one ever will, which makes it such a perfect New Labour word: it sounds business-like, positive and scientific, while yet being so ambiguous as to be meaningless.

So when the government announces it plans to 'roll out an initiative', what it's actually saying is, 'not in your lifetime, mate'.

Routemaster Bus

It was a design classic uniquely suited to London's streets. Everyone loved it. You could hop on and off whenever you wanted. You could stand on the platform, grab on to the pole and lean out with the wind in your face. There was a conductor on board to help you feel safe and dispense homespun West-Indian charm, which is more than your typical harassed bus driver is willing, or able, to do. It transformed an ordinary journey by public transport into something liberating and enjoyable with just the slightest frisson of devil-may-care risk. The Routemaster bus was durable, handsome, efficient, popular and fun. 'Only some ghastly dehumanised moron would want to get rid of the Routemaster,' Ken Livingstone correctly observed in 2001 – which is why he had to ban it, obviously.

RSPB

Legitimised animal rights terror organisation with values more in tune with the politically correct animal rights lobby than with gamekeepers or conservationists. A bit like the RSPCA (see opposite), except that because hardly any of us keep budgies or parrots – psittcosis? bird poo on our heads? no, thanks – about the only people it gets to pick on are toffy landowners.

Its especial pleasure is nabbing gamekeepers on grouse-shooting estates for destroying bird of prey eggs. The thinking being, presumably, that because all birds of prey are magnificent, soaring specimens with glinting eyes, sharp beaks, and other splendid Ted Hughes-type qualities, they must perforce be the best thing since sliced bread and deserving of preservation at all costs.

What this sentimental notion fails to recognise, though, is that nature is not in fact a very natural thing. The reason our land-scape, our flora and our fauna are the way they are is because generations of landowners have shaped them for a particular purpose. We have stone walls and hedges rather than barbed wire, because hunting folk find them better for jumping over. We have patchwork-patterned grouse moors because the heather has to be deliberately burnt at intervals to encourage new growth for young birds to thrive; we have lots of grouse on those managed moors because the predators (foxes and, yes, birds like ravens and goshawks) are kept in check by gamekeepers.

Which is why, funnily enough, research has shown that land managed by gamekeepers for shooting is generally much better run, with greater biodiversity than land run on more PC lines by the RSPB. On the grouse moors of the North Pennines, for example, the curlew has increased eighteen times more than in the Berwyn Special Protection Area, which is run as an RSPB nature reserve.

So really, what the RSPB ought to be doing is running its nature reserves as shooting estates. Bill Oddie might be a bit pissed off. But at two thousand quid per gun per day they could probably afford not to care.

RSPCA (see also Crayfish)

Once a loveable, kindly, harmless organisation – the charity you could always spare a few coppers for because of the wonderful work it did with sick puppies and tired ponies and kittens with bandaged paws – the RSPCA now seems more like the State-sanctioned Gestapo of the animal rights lobby. It wants to ban everything from fox hunting to fairground goldfish. Its uniformed inspectors will boot down your door at the slightest animal rights violation, be it a fish tank whose glass has gone slightly green or the fat, farting labrador you have been seen to turf out of the room with excessive enthusiasm.

Consider the case of the policeman who, in the absence of any vets, chose to put a dying cat out of its misery by whacking it over the head. The RSPCA spent two years and £50,000 (imagine how much more fun those 50,000 little old ladies might have had if they'd spent their donation on a lottery ticket instead) pursuing this ruthless cat-abuser through the courts, only to have the case thrown out by a judge. An organisation as zealous as that isn't going to remain content with cats and dogs and bunnies and goldfish is it?

Any day now, they'll be agitating for a new code of protection for sewer rats and mice. Then it will be wasps and slugs. Then houseflies. Then fleas and midges. Then you won't even be allowed to wash your bed-linen any more, in case you damage the precious dust mites.

S

Salt (see also Vegans; Vegetarians)

'There's no salt in the casserole so would you mind adding your own? I'm afraid I've got out of the habit because of the kids.'

What? And because you've got into this stupid habit for your kids' sake that automatically lets you off the hook for having served me crap food at dinner, does it?

Well I'm sorry Mrs ditzy, health-scare-credulous middle-class dinner party hostess but no it sodding well doesn't.

Suppose we were to go to dinner at Gordon Ramsay's or Le Manoir aux Quat'Saisons. What do you reckon the chances might be of our finding a note on the menu saying: 'In response to consumer demand and mindful of health and safety (*qv*) issues, chef has decided that from now on he will stop seasoning his dishes.' Pretty slim, I reckon. Not a snowball's chance in hell in fact. Why? Because Gordon Ramsay and Raymond Blanc and any other chef you could name who's worth his salt – there's a clue – understands a very basic truth about cooking: unless it's properly seasoned you might as well not bother.

It's not a personal taste thing either. It's not a case of, 'one person's oversalted, is another person's undersalted'. Go to any of the world's great kitchens and you'll find a remarkable degree of consistency in the amount of salt used in the cooking. It's one of the chef de cuisine's most important jobs, continually having little tastes from the battery of bubbling pots to ensure his various commis chefs and sous chefs have got their seasoning exactly right. That's why, when you go to a properly run restaurant, you will never eat a dish that tastes too salty. Nor will you eat one where you need to sprinkle on a bit more.

So if this rule is good enough for the great masters of cuisine (and mistresses – because I'll bet Pru Leith or Nigella don't have any silly salt hang-ups), why, pray, is it not good enough for you? Or, more importantly, for your dinner guests?

Actually don't tell me. I know. You've been reading the propaganda, all of it undiscriminatingly repeated by newspapers that really aren't bothered whether it's true or not, just so long as it gives the readers a juicy new health scare to set their panic alarms going, that's the important thing.

You'll be aware then of the government guidelines that we should all eat no more than a teaspoon of salt per day. And that ideally we shouldn't be feeding our children any salt at all.

But what you probably won't be aware of is that it's all basically rubbish. Yes a famous eighties study did show that if you feed chimpanzees fifteen times their normal salt intake they end up with high blood pressure. (If you fed them fifteen times their normal dose of anything – bananas; PG Tips – you'd probably get the same result.) Yes, if you suffer from hypertension, you do need a low-salt diet. True, salt isn't good for babies. The rest, though, is pure nanny state busybodying.

There is no consistent scientific evidence to show that a state-enforced reduction in our salt intake would make a significant difference to the health of the nation. What it would most definitely do, though, is to take the government into areas of our lives where it has absolutely no business to be.

Unless you fit into a particularly vulnerable category (if, for example, your children are in fact slugs. Check now: do they look like stubby lengths of grey or black or white gelatinous slime, with feelers on the end? If so, yes, avoid giving them salt), drastically reducing the amount of salt in your diet will not make the slightest difference to how long you'll live or how healthy you feel. And the same applies to your kids.

What it will do for sure, though, is stop your food tasting as good as it ought to. It will also teach your children that healthy home cooking doesn't taste nearly as nice as the Pot Noodles and crisps they get at their friends' houses. And they will grow up without a properly trained palate, thus killing their chances of ever getting three Michelin stars. Or even landing a job in the local greasy spoon.

Schoolgirls Dressed In Jilbabs

Some things were always meant to be: ravens in the Tower of London; lamb with mint sauce; crocodiles of schoolgirls in proper schoolgirl uniform of stripy ties, white blouses, dark tights and very short skirts. There's nothing pervy about it (well not much). It's the English way and has been since at least St Trinian's.

How dispiriting, then, that in 2005 a Luton schoolgirl named Shabina Begum, should have been encouraged to spend thousands of taxpayers' pounds campaigning for her 'right' to turn up to school with her beautiful face masked by what Muslims call a jilbab. Or, as the commentator Rod Liddle more trenchantly put it, by 'a top to toe expanse of hessian sacking with a small aperture for part of her face'.

There were many disturbing aspects to the Shabina Begum case. One was the hearty endorsement it got from Hizb-ut-Tahrir, the extremist organisation founded by the drooling self-publicist and inflammatory preacher 'Sheikh' Omar Bakri Mohammed who has endorsed suicide bombings and encouraged British Muslims to join al-Qaeda. (But who still thought it jolly unfair when British warships refused to evacuate him from war-torn Lebanon in August 2006 on account of his being such a treacherous tosser.)

Another was the utter spinelessness shown by the Court of Appeal which in my view, by deciding in the girl's favour, announced itself perfectly happy to surrender liberal, secular values to those of bullying Islamism. (A decision which, in an uncharacteristic fit of commonsense, the Law Lords subsequently reversed.)

Yet another was the fact that Shabina's counsel in the final case was one Cherie Booth. While it might not be fair to blame Ms Booth for taking on the case – barristers do have to operate on the cab rank principle – it surely cannot be healthy that the wife of a serving prime minister should be acting in a cause widely perceived to be flagrantly at odds with the national interest.

But by far the most depressing aspect of the case – as Liddle was one of the few commentators brave and clear-sighted enough to appreciate – was that while Britain may have won the Shabina Begum battle, it has long since lost the broader cultural war to defend secular values against Islamic fundamentalism.

Already – after consultation with mosques and community leaders (qv) – schools all over Britain are permitting Muslim girls to turn up in modesty-protecting uniforms only marginally more revealing than the one demanded by Shabina. In the name of 'multiculturalism' (qv), in other words, our state education system is now cheerfully endorsing the sexism, intolerance and inequality that generations of feminists and liberal thinkers have spent the last hundred years fighting so hard to curtail.

Scoper

Never more exquisitely was the road to hell paved with good intentions than when the Spastics Society – a charity for victims of cerebral palsy – decided to change its name to SCOPE. The society had discovered that 'spastic', 'spazzer' and 'spazzmo' – usually accompanied by flailing arm gestures and the pushing-out of one's lower jaw with one's tongue – were all common forms of playground abuse for children who showed vague signs of malcoordination, incompetence, ugliness, unpopularity or general all-round spasticity.

Clearly this prejudice (*qv*) and injustice would have to be remedied with a multi-million-pound rebranding exercise. And so SCOPE was born. Sure enough, schoolchildren hardly ever call one another 'spastic' any more. They call each other 'Scoper' instead.

Seacole, Mary (see also Diwali; Environment, The; Litter)

Principal topic at all state primary schools.

Silent Spring

Ask any environmentalist of a certain age what it was that set them on the path to enlightenment and they'll tell you it was Rachel Carson's landmark 1962 bestseller *Silent Spring*. Everyone read it, and almost everyone believed its apocalyptic predictions of a cancer epidemic that could hit 'practically one hundred per cent' of the human population and of birdlife being wiped out – all because of man's use of the deadly insecticide DDT. This makes the poster girl of the eco movement one of the twentieth-century's worst mass-murderers. By effecting the ban on DDT Carson deprived the developing world of its most cost-effective control against mosquitoes, leading to millions of quite unnecessary deaths from malaria. This is why the ban was recently rescinded by the World Health Organisation.

Maybe, if there had been a scintilla of truth in *Silent Spring*'s claims, those deaths might be considered somehow justified. Problem is, pretty much everything the book said was nonsense. DDT doesn't cause cancer. It doesn't, *pace* Carson, damage bird reproduction. Carson's brand of junk science and misanthropic, anti-capitalist doom-mongering has provided the model for the international green movement ever since.

Smoking, Numerous Arguments In Favour Of, The

Smoking kills. But then, so do fast cars, drink, drugs, sex, great white sharks, black mambas, MiG-35s, Challenger II tanks, AH 64 attack helicopters, Uzis and daisycutter bombs, and are we supposed to ban them as well?

Actually don't answer that question, any of you health and safety zealots out there, because I know what you're going to say already. 'Yes, yes, yes! Ban them all! Ban everything that's fun! Ban everything that's dangerous! Ban everything that's sexy and exciting and edgy and cool! In fact don't stop banning things till the only thing left to do is sip room-temperature water from a cup made of splinter-free sustainable wood, eat tofu and watch grass grow (taking care to do so in the shade between 10 a.m. and 3 p.m. and while wearing organic, non-allergenic, sun cream of SPF50 or higher, obviously)...'

Smoking kills and smoking is fun. The fact that smoking kills is an integral part of that fun. Of course, smoking has lots of other things going for it too, including:

it gives you a delicious quivery rush – especially when you've not had a fag in a while because you stupidly tried to give up but have now seen the light; it goes fantastically well with coffee and alcohol and cocaine and stressful phone conversations; or happy, upbeat phone conversations; and in-between phone conversations; it's fantastic after sex; it's the best cure for pre-party nerves; it helps you bond with other smokers who, being addictive type-A personalities, are inevitably more interesting than non-smokers; it stops you getting Alzheimer's disease, some research claimed once; it enhances perfect moments; it wards off boredom, kills time, and gives you something to do with your hands; it improves your origami skills and enables you to stun friends with the brilliant rose flower you have managed to craft from the packet's gold foil; it means you've usually got a light or cigarettes on you, which might come in handy in unexpected survival situations; it means if you haven't got a light you're going to meet new people; it boosts the livelihood of tobacco growers in the third world and North Carolina; it wards off mosquitoes, midges, gnats, wasps and flies; it masks the smell of farts; it provides you with an excuse to escape awkward conversations at parties and speak to people you'd like to speak to instead; it enables you to nip out of the office for some fresh air and some gossip; it winds up puritans and health freaks; it provides instant solace in extremis (war, firing squads, etc.); it helps you befriend grizzled peasants in Greek mountain villages, South American rebels, Chinese steel-workers and a billion and one other types with whom you have nothing linguistically in common; it gives you a sexy, husky voice; it helps you concentrate; it makes you feel like James Dean, Humphrey Bogart, Steve McQueen; Lauren Bacall; Marlene Dietrich; Isambard Kingdom Brunel; Groucho Marx;

Winston Churchill; Clint Eastwood and anyone else in history who ever looked good with a fag or cigar or a stogie, which is pretty much everybody who smokes.

Extraordinary to think that we're banning these things. We should be making them compulsory.

Social Workers

Come the revolution, the social workers will be the first to your door, rounding up your kids, replacing all their nice Boden clothes with hessian sacks and all their Horrid Henry books with badly illustrated, dog-eared library copies of well-loved West Indian Folk Tales featuring Anansie the Spider, and dragging them off to be turned into young lesbians, homosexuals and communists by their new foster parents at the political re-education camp.

Most social workers bitterly regret that they were not around in the days of Stalin's Soviet Union when, of course, they would have been the political commissars whose noble job it was during the war to wait in the rear of the frontline with machine guns, ready to mow down any bourgeois reactionaries in their army who tried to retreat.

This dream job opportunity no longer being available, social workers now live in hope of achieving the next best thing on their all-time wish-list: elbowing their way into the lives of a nice middle-class family and completely destroying it.

See, the problem with middle-class scum is that – unlike the cowed, battered council-estate families social workers normally deal with – they have far too much money and freedom of choice, and like to see themselves as being beyond the apparatus of state control which social workers believe should be compulsory for everyone.

But how to bag that coveted middle-class scalp, that's the problem. One option is to try to nick them for ritual Satanic abuse. After Orkney and Cleveland, though, this method is looking a bit risky.

So, ideally, what they need is one of those cases where, say, the baby's fallen off the bed and bumped its head. Then they can find an 'expert' to show that this is consistent with violent shaking by either the father or the mother. The child can be removed from the family's care. Serve them right for being so smug. And what do families know about bringing up children, anyway? All those terrible bourgeois reactionary values they teach them, really, it's a disgrace. Leave child-rearing to the experts. To the social workers!

Sounds To Curdle The Blood

1. Tony Blair's emotional catches-in-the-throat as he reads the lesson at the Princess of Wales's funeral.
2. The bearded fellow with the rucksack next to you on the tube suddenly yelling, 'Allahu Akhbar!'
3. The Tory party conference's smug murmurs of assent at a screening of Al Gore's *An Inconvenient Truth*.
4. The especially loud applause that inevitably breaks out on *Question Time* after one of the panellists has daringly and originally spoken out against the Iraq war.
5. 'Over to you Ekow Eshun...'

Spanish, The

The Spanish have an awful lot going for them. They have no vegetables whatsoever in their diet – just beef, pig and octopus; their culture – fighting bulls, chucking donkeys from the tops of towers, having Moors and Christians festivals – is heroically un-PC;

they provide a happy retirement home for down-on-their-luck Britons such as East End gangsters, Howard Marks and David Beckham; and, above all, they're not French.

However, our Spanish chums' general splendour should never be allowed to blind us to their manifest faults, *viz*: they have huge trawler fleets at least a billion times the size of ours which steal all our fish and have wiped every single species within a hundred miles of our shores from the largest blue whale to the tiniest plankton; they've utterly destroyed one of the Med's prettiest coastlines with tower blocks and illegally built villas (each one of which has been sold to about half-a-dozen different English retirees who are in for a nasty shock when they finally inspect the title deeds) and they simply don't care because they think nature is something fit only to be raped and plundered and obliterated quicker than you can say Quetzalcoatl; they completely blew the challenge proffered by the Madrid train bombings, replacing a government of conviction with a surrender-monkey lefty one and sending a clear message to Islamists everywhere – 'Oh all right then. Do roll all over us, restore the Caliphate and reclaim Al Andaluz. We always thought that El Cid bloke was overrated anyway.'

Speed Cameras

It's 3 a.m., a clear, dry summer's morning and you're feeling great. The road to the coast is completely clear, you've beaten the holiday traffic, you've got some killer driving music on your stereo: under the circumstances, would it not be an absolute crime not to floor the accelerator and see what your baby's made of?

Ten seconds later: BLAP!

'Ohmygod. Was that a flash? It was a flash. It was a flash. What was I doing? Fuck! That's just gone and cost me my licence.'

So let's get this right. We are the country which invented British racing green, the Bentley Mulsanne turbo and the E-type Jag; we produced Malcolm and Donald Campbell, Graham Hill, Jackie Stewart, James Hunt, Nigel Mansell and Jeremy Clarkson; we're the home of Silverstone, Brands Hatch and the Formula One race industry; our national TV programme is *Top Gear*. Yet, somehow, we've allowed all our driving freedoms little by little to be stolen away from us by the stunted, car-hating kill-joys of the health and safety lobby.

Never again will we be truly able to enjoy the thrill of the open road, nor drive our cars at the speeds for which they were designed, nor, frankly, ever enjoy another car journey in our miserable oppressed lives. Like some hideous, bloated fun-leech, the safety Nazis have sucked every last drop of joy from our travels.

Ten years ago there were fewer than a hundred speed cameras on the roads. Now there are more than 6,000. They raise £120 million in fines, so it's not as though the police or the local authorities have much incentive to stop this terrible blight.

Is the only answer then for us all to grab a chainsaw and hack the bastards down wheresoever they may be? You may think that, but obviously I couldn't possibly say.

Speed Kills

No it doesn't, usually – whatever they may tell you on those horrid little speeding workshop courses you can attend in lieu of losing yet more points off your licence. In fact, according to Department for Transport (DfT) figures published in September 2005, the number of accidents involving motorists breaking the speed limit is only 5 per cent. 'Ah,' say the anti-speed fanatics. 'But excessive speed can turn a bad accident into an even worse one.' Yes, and if everyone were to remain stationary in their cars, in their garages, with the engine off, the number of road traffic accidents would decrease by 100 per cent.

Spooks (see also Drug Dealer, Evil, International)

There isn't really an Islamist terror threat, you know. It says so on BBC1's incredibly authentic spy series, *Spooks*. When one of the spy chiefs talks about 'Muslim terror', he makes little inverted commas signs with his fingers to show that, of course, the concept is an outrageous calumny on such a universally peace-loving community. When there's a plot involving Middle Eastern hijackers who take over a London embassy and shoot people every hour, they turn out, inevitably, to be Jews in disguise. And when a group of suicidal religious extremists launch grenade and bomb attacks on the innocent members of another faith, the baddies turn out to be fundamentalist Christians and the goodies, yes, Muslims. Goodness, where would we be without the BBC and its courageous, unswerving adherence to the round, unvarnished truth?

Statistics We Do Not Care About

'Britain imprisons a higher percentage of its population than any other Western European country.'

Oh, dear. Well, that's my day ruined then. The thought of all those criminals locked up when they could be out on the streets mugging, burgling, raping, murdering fair tugs at the heart strings, it really does. Let's free half of them right now. Sure it might involve one or two more of us being stabbed to death in side alleys or sprayed with an Uzi in drive-by shootings, but at least we could hold our heads up high on the really important issue: where

Britain stands in the international niceness leagues of bleeding-heart sociology.

The trouble with this statistical factoid, tirelessly trotted out as the ultimate proof of Britain's fascistic prison policy, is that it is quite meaningless. Why? Because it takes no account of the fact that we have a higher proportion of thieves, thugs, psychos and other criminal ne'er-do-wells than almost every other country on the planet. Once you take into account Britain's extraordinary criminality (i.e. crimes per head of population) a very different figure emerges. While Britain imprisons just 12 people per 1,000 crimes, Spain imprisons 48 and Ireland 33. Only Sweden, with 4.7 prisoners per 1000 crimes, has a lower incarceration rate. And yes, by spooky coincidence, Sweden and Britain have the two highest rates of recorded crime in Europe.

So let's build more prisons, quick. We've got an awful lot of catching up to do.

Steel, Mark

See Thomas, Mark.

Stern Report

In years to come people are going to look back on the Stern Report (if anyone remembers it at all, that is) rather as we might now view an eighteenth-century share prospectus for the South Sea Company. 'Surely no one actually believed that guff?' shivering children will ask their teachers, as yet another large glacier with hundreds of polar bears on top creeps past their classroom window. 'Ah well,' their wise history teacher (presuming that such people actually exist in the future) will reply. 'What you have to realise, children, is that in those benighted days global-warming hysteria had spread like a virus from which not even clever civil servants nor Tory leaders with first-class degrees from Oxford were immune. By the time the bubble burst and man-made climate-change was exposed as just another fad, the money had already been spent. This, dear children, is why you live in igloos rather than the lovely, centrally heated houses you would have had if the global economy hadn't been so royally shafted . . .'

Sting (see also Coldplay)

Obviously, with all those tantric yoga skills he must have mastered the art of auto-fellatio years ago but has he yet developed the ability to kiss his own arse?

T

Tate Britain/Tate Modern

Smiths; Move; Sudan; King's Road; Black Death; Right Stuff; Tate; The. None of them sounds nearly as good without a 'The' in front. The 'the' lends them gravitas; singularity; familiarity; resonance. When you walk down the King's Road you're buying into layer upon layer of social history – the Picasso café, the Duke of York's barracks, R Soles, Johnny Moke, Vivienne Westwood at World's End. When you walk down King's Road, it becomes just another modern high street swamped with Starbucks and Costa coffee houses.

But this, of course, is exactly what progressives would like to achieve. They prefer 'Sudan' to 'the Sudan' because it sounds less colonial. They prefer 'Tate Britain' to 'the Tate' because it sounds more vibrant and contemporary – less redolent of nicely spoken families being edified by Turners and Constables on a wet Sunday afternoon. The fact is that progressives find it shameful and retrograde that galleries still tend to be full of paintings collected by elitist, rich people and appreciated mainly by well-educated white people. It doesn't quite fit in with their drive to improve 'access' (*qv*) at all costs.

Wherever possible, do make sure you taunt these progressives by referring fogeyishly to 'the Tate'. Not only will it signify your rejection of the modish Tate Britain, but it will also hint that you really don't think all that much of the trendy nonsense they show in that converted power station south of the river, you know the one – where they exhibit all those white painted boxes, decaying animal carcasses and such like – oh really, what on earth is its name?

Thatcher, Margaret

If it hadn't been for Margaret Thatcher, Britain would now be languishing in the international economic league tables somewhere between Albania and Burkina Faso. She made a sick, sclerotic Britain great again, something which in 1979 was by no means a foregone conclusion. Yet even at her peak she never had popularity ratings to rival Tony Blair's and today it still requires a certain courage to acknowledge openly what an extraordinary woman you think she was. Another puzzling question (*qv* Blair, Tony) for the historians, then.

Thomas, Mark

See Steel, Mark

Tom and Jerry

Kids: feel free to whack your friends' faces with frying pans until they're completely flat; to drop ten-ton weights on their heads; to smash them with hammers and axes; and to shove down their throats an accordion which then expands to create an amusing, bellows-like zigzag effect. But don't, whatever you do, think to follow the cat's noxious example from a 1950s episode of *Tom and Jerry* in which – heaven forfend – he is actually depicted rolling a cigarette. Not that you would anyway. After consultation in 2006 with the media watchdog Ofcom, the children's channel

Boomerang has now decided to edit out all scenes which might in any way be seen to condone such disgusting, dangerous practices.

Toynbee, Polly (see also Why Oh Why?)

New Tory role model, greater even than Winston Churchill, apparently (see Cameron, Dave)

Traffic Wardens

Traffic wardens. We've always hated the bastards, of course. But where once we might have found space amid our general loathing grudgingly to admit that they were only doing their job and that if they weren't there the streets would be a chaos of double-parked cars and jammed traffic, today those excuses no longer apply. Apart, maybe, from the tiny Amazonian fish that swims up your urine stream and can only be extracted when you've chopped your penis off, the modern British traffic warden must surely qualify as the most loathsome species on the planet.

You could, of course, argue that it's their employers' fault. Ever since local councils cottoned on to the fact that it's far easier to raise revenue by stinging law-abiding, tax-paying motorists than it is persuading inbreeds, rent-dodgers, spongers and criminals to pay for the services they so cheerfully exploit, traffic wardens have been put under tremendous pressure to ticket as many parking offenders as they possibly can. Those that fail to fulfil their quota lose their jobs, so it's quite understandable that they pursue their task with such remorseless zeal.

Understandable, yes; forgivable, no. For, in their desperation to keep their miserable, vile jobs, they allow all standards of fairness and decency to fly out of the window. Which of us has not experienced the pullulating, helpless, day-ruining rage which comes from returning to the car we've parked quite legitimately, only to discover stuck to the windscreen a demand for the whopping sum of £100 (which hey, the council will generously reduce to a mere £50 if you pay within the requisite period)?

Hmm. Which trumped-up offence has the traffic warden devised this time? Perhaps, we've failed to stick the ticket so indisputably bang in the middle on the driver's side of the windscreen that he (it is mostly a 'he' these days) can try claiming it wasn't 'clearly displayed'. Or maybe he's chosen to ignore our huge note explaining that the broken ticket machine has swallowed all our money and we're off to get some more change and find a machine that works. Or maybe he's decided that part of our vehicle is protruding by a fraction of a millimetre beyond its officially allotted parking space. Or maybe he's noticed nothing wrong at all and thought, 'What the hell, I'll give them a ticket anyway. Chances are, they won't bother to contest.'

And just to rub salt into the wound, the parking authorities have a final cruel trick to play. They won't deal with your complaint till after the period for 'reduced-rate payment' has elapsed, which means that instead of being stung fifty quid for the ticket you should never have had anyway, you run the risk of having to fork out £100. A lot of victims decide at this point to cut their losses, pay the fifty and forget about it. Which, of course, is just why the parking authorities introduced this nasty little clause. And why so many traffic wardens can get away with issuing so many unfair tickets.

Every now and then, after one scandalised newspaper report too many, councils like to announce that in future they are going to rein in their traffic wardens' excesses. But they never do. For one thing, such easy money is too tempting to resist for long. And for another, if they did things by the book they just wouldn't raise enough revenue. Because of the number of traffic wardens and the scale of the fines, very few drivers are so rich or stupid these days as to park illegally by choice. And if drivers will insist on parking inside the law, what option does a hard-working traffic warden have but to scribble away and drag them, kicking and screaming, outside it?

Travellers v Gypsies

So let me get this right. Travellers are the ones who: steal your lawnmower; poo in your hedgerow; burgle your property; toss rubbish in your back garden; dump their rusty cars in your lane; annexe the neighbouring fields; halve the value of your property; raise their urchins to be so poisonous and contemptuous of discipline that the moment they enrol en masse at your local primary school every other child and parent in the neighbourhood wants to flee; illegally colonise your local greenfield site, cover it with hardcore, divide it into rubbish-strewn plots, erect ugly, jerry-built houses on it in defiance of planning regulations and then refuse to budge, claiming human rights (qv); force your council to spend millions trying to evict them; make false benefit claims; scream abuse at you; keep you awake at night with the barking of their aggressive, mangy dogs; make life utter, abject misery for anyone unfortunate enough to be living in the area where they choose to settle.

And gypsies are the ones who: live in wonderful painted caravans; exude a delightful roving spirit; have numerous fine old Romany traditions such as fortune telling, bareknuckle boxing and the special language known as cant which gives us the word 'chav'; feature prominently and charmingly in Rupert Bear annuals, Sunday evening cosy village dramas and Philip Pullman's *Northern Lights*.

Or is it the other way round?

Trees Don't Rape

Typically silly message daubed on a tree in Hyde Park at a Stop Climate Chaos rally. Nor do trees: cure cancer, write poetry, cook fabulous dinners, form loving relationships, teach children right from wrong or wrestle stricken passenger jets to the ground when they've been hit by lightning and for several tense minutes it seems as if everyone aboard is going to die.

Two-Minute Silence

A perennial annoyance when reading new one hundred greatest albums of all time polls is noticing how masterpieces like *Led Zeppelin IV* or Neil Young's *Harvest* are forever being elbowed out of the Top Twenty by Robbie Williams, Kaiser Chiefs or the latest boy band purely because the idiot kids who vote for these lists lack the historical perspective to understand the difference between the enduring and the ephemeral. A similar mentality appears to have afflicted the government in its cavalier treatment of the two-minute silence.

Since 1919, the two-minute silence on the eleventh hour of the eleventh day of the eleventh month has been used to commemorate the innumerable dead of the First and, later, the Second World War. To insist, as the government did in 2005 and 2006, that we hold a separate two-minute silence in July to commemorate the victims of the 7/7 London suicide bombings, defeats the object of the exercise.

For one thing, it cheapens the currency. Around 800,000 British soldiers were killed or posted missing during the First World War, nearly 20,000 of them in the first day of the Battle of the Somme; another 450,000 British soldiers and civilians were killed during the Second World War – at least 40,000 in the Blitz bombing raids. Fifty-two people were killed during the 7/7 bombings in 2005 – horrible of course – but not quite in the same league of awfulness.

A more worrying problem, though, is that 7/7 most certainly won't be the last Islamist atrocity on British soil, nor will it be the most deadly. So what will the government have us do when the next, bigger one comes? Are we to commemorate it with four minutes' silence? Ten minutes' silence? A whole week's worth?

Or might it not perhaps be a better use of our time for all of us to spend a few moments thinking very, very hard about how it came to pass that a section of our population now finds it socially and morally justifiable to try to murder as many of the rest of us as it can. And then thinking even harder about what we might do to prevent such a thing happening again. Something a bit more forthright and practical, let's hope, than standing quietly for a couple of minutes not meeting anybody's eye and feeling slightly awkward.

Typhoon Eurofighter

You're a squaddie holed up in a dismal, dust-blown outpost somewhere in Helmand province: food's dire; flies everywhere; diarrhoea positively Niagran. Day after day you're under attack from the Taliban who are throwing everything they've got at you. Not since Korea has the British army had this much intense combat experience. You should have been rotated out of this dump weeks ago, but there aren't sufficient replacements. You'd like to email home but you can't, the system's down, in fact everything's breaking down out here: helicopters; Nimrods; supply vehicles. When you finally head home there's no certainty you're going to make it in one piece: not when you're travelling in Snatch Land Rovers which offer almost no protection against the main local hazards – mines, suicide bombs, IEDs, RPGs. For this you're being paid £2.45 an hour.

But never mind all that, here's the really important thing: some time in the distant future it's all going to be OK, because your air force is going to take delivery of some really spiffy new fighters – none of your much cheaper, much more effective, combat-proven American rubbish; proper pan-European jobs these are – which are going to be absolutely fab at fighting the Soviet Union when its tanks start rolling across Lüneburg Heath.

No. Wait. The Soviet Union doesn't actually exist any more. Which means . . .

Oh bugger. Never mind. It's only £20 billion down the drain.

U

'Uni'

It's easy to tell whether or not someone has had an education: if they have, they call it university; if they haven't, they call it uni.

Uni is the place you go to drink, shag and puke your way through around £20,000-worth of borrowed money, provided at a special low interest rate courtesy of the taxpayer.

University was the place where you used to do exactly the same but with two crucial differences. One, you were lucky enough to do so without incurring much debt because in that happy era your further education was paid for by the state. Two, the degree you got at the end actually counted for something (see also Polytechnics).

So where did it all go wrong? Why, possibly when Mrs Thatcher decided in one of her more hare-brained moments to allow polytechnics to rebrand themselves as universities. But more damagingly at the point where Tony Blair dreamed up the brilliant scheme of boosting the country's university population from 15 per cent of school leavers to 50 per cent. Apparently, in the future, Britain would have a lot more vacancies for 'graduate-level' jobs.

Quite possibly it will. Unfortunately, in order to meet Mr Blair's target, our universities have had to dumb down their courses to such idiot-friendly levels the degrees they now offer are barely worth having. So employers are hardly going to be looking for British 'uni' graduates to fill all those graduate-level jobs. They'll be looking for the ones who had a proper education. In some foreign country, no doubt, where they still call uni university.

Uniformed Border Control Officers

Immigration is spinning out of control and not even the Home Office has the faintest idea how many illegals have entered the country, but at last the government has a plan. In its ambitiously titled policy document *Rebuilding Confidence In Our Immigration System*, it proposes that instead of wearing plain clothes, passport control officers should wear a uniform. 'Zzzplidj!' you can just imagine those Albanians saying: 'I was planning on coming to England to set up a new gangster network. But now I see from those new navy blue uniforms, perhaps with discreet but stylish red and white piping designed by Jeff Banks, that from now on the British mean business about immigration. I shall try somewhere else instead.'

United Nations

For every international problem the world's bleeding hearts have the same solution: 'Send in the UN.' I wonder – are we talking about the same organisation? The UN they keep banging on about would appear to be a wise, just and widely respected international body with the power to resolve the world's most intractable problems through a combination of clever negotiating skills and judicious force. But the only UN I know of is a shambles of corruption, venality, muddled thinking, needless waste, political correctness and monumental incompetence. Barely an outfit you'd trust to run a brewery piss-up or even your bath, let alone put in charge of such chewy issues as Iran's nuclear weapons programme or the policing of the Lebanon.

Let's suppose, for a moment, that we do mean the same UN and have a look at some of its recent achievements. Hmm, yes, there was the unfortunate revelation that its officials in the Congo have been running paedophile rings, raping children and using them as prostitutes.

And the 1994 genocide in Rwanda when, despite protests from the peacekeepers' local commander Romeo Dallaire, the UN withdrew almost all its troops enabling around 937,000 Tutsis and moderate Hutus to be slaughtered by the Interahamwe.

And the small matter of Srebrenica in 1995 where more of those feared and respected pale-blue-helmet troops – Dutch ones this time – were charged with the protection of local Bosnians in an official UN safe haven. Only to discover the next day: 'Well bugger me! It seems that 8,000 men and boys have just been wiped out by the Serbs.'*

And the glorious occasion when the UN was voting on new member states for its human rights commission and elected Libya and the Sudan. Yes, Libya as in the place which masterminded the Lockerbie bombing; and the Sudan, as in thousands of innocent men, women and children in Darfur province being massacred by the Janjaweed as part of a state-sponsored exercise in ethnic cleansing.

I see. And this is the organisation you think we should be trusting to make the world a safer place, do you, all you *Guardian*- and *Independent*-readers out there?

You'll be telling me next that if only we'd left the UN to sort out Saddam, we would never have had the current mess in Iraq. But what you'd be forgetting there, perhaps, is that it was the UN that got us into that mess in the first place. Not only did the UN senior employees help bolster Saddam's regime and increase the suffering of Iraq's people with their multi-billion-dollar 'oil for fraud' scam, but the UN proved itself pathetically reluctant to enforce any of the resolutions it had imposed on Iraq, forcing a frustrated US and its allies to do the job themselves. Similar rules applied in Lebanon in August 2006. The Hezbollah forces that Israel tried to evict from southern Lebanon would never even have been there if the UN was serious about enforcing its resolutions.

Of course, the real reason the left so adores the UN is not because it works but because it so infuriates the Americans. In the old days, it did this by enabling China and Russia to frustrate US foreign policy by vetoing its every resolution. More recently, it has enabled all the world's banana republics, squalid dictatorships, African kleptocracies, communist basket cases and Muslim theocracies to form a power bloc in which they can cheerfully oppose any resolution that threatens to further the cause of peace, prosperity and common sense.

John Bolton, the US Ambassador to the UN once famously observed: 'The [UN] secretariat building in New York has thirty-eight stories. If it lost ten stories it wouldn't make a bit of difference.'

Hey, why stop at ten?

*For which they were subsequently given medals by the Dutch government, so as to spare them any possible hurt feelings.

Vegans

Sweaty-shoed, no-fun vegetarians who can't even have honey and butter on toast.

Vegetarians

Once, they knew their place. They'd eat up all the potatoes and cabbage round the hunk of bleeding steak you'd given them, and not mind too much about the essence of dead animal they'd inevitably consumed because, hey, that was the price they deserved to pay for having such weird, pervy, dietary habits.

Ever since they became a single-issue power bloc, though, they've got much more uppity. They won't let you warm up their Linda McCartney veg-o-stew in the pan you used to fry the bacon; they get all upset when you tell them that the secret of the delicious veggie broth they've just eaten is really good chicken stock; and they now actually expect you to prepare a special vegetarian main course for them when they come to dinner, claiming the bowl of rice and soy sauce you gave them last time didn't quite hit the spot.

Listen, veggies, the only reason you're here at all is because your ancestors ate sufficient quantities of meat to enable their brains to grow at stupendous rates, thus ensuring man – rather than, say, sheep or butterflies (which I know you'd prefer to be, but tough) – became the dominant species. And anyway, you know you love bacon really.

Victim

Until quite recently a victim was something you definitely didn't want to be. Most commonly, you were the victim of a mugging; or if you were really unlucky, a murder victim. Pictures of you would appear in newspapers, wearing a gown and smiling in your university graduation portrait, and readers would shake their heads and think what a tragedy it was that you'd been cut down in your prime when you'd clearly shown so much promise.

You could also have been a car crash victim, an AIDS victim, a victim of circumstance and a victim of mistaken identity – none of which was a particularly desirable thing to be. Today, though, if you can't be a professional footballer, a pop star, or the winner of *Big Brother*, becoming a victim is about the best career move going. Victims make more money (lavish compensation, selling stories to newspapers, etc.), get better jobs (positive discrimination), get more respect (victimhood equals authenticity) and more power. What's more they've the perfect excuse to write one of those lucrative misery memoirs (*qv*) which just seem to fly off the shelves these days.

There are now six victim groups officially recognised by the state and granted special protection status: women; ethnic minorities; the disabled; non-Christians; the elderly; homosexuals. According to the think tank Civitas, this means that 73 per cent of the population can claim to be victimised. And the other 27 per cent of us, presumably, to claim that we are now part of an oppressed, beleaguered and discriminated-against minority.

W

Water

Think you're ever going to be allowed to use a hose pipe ever again? Dream on. There are now parts of Britain where there is less water per head of population than in the deserts of the Sudan but this has little to do with global warming, freak droughts, antiquated water pipes or any of the other excuses routinely trotted out by our useless, profiteering water companies. It's mostly down to the bizarre, almost Stalinist rationing system by which our water supply is allocated.

We're all quite used to the idea by now of paying for the amount of gas and electricity we use, and the quantities of foie gras we eat, and the number of pints of beer we drink, and so on. Yet still – rather like with health and the NHS (qv) – there seems to be an idea abroad that water is such a special commodity it should be left to the state to decide how much we get.

Though our water industry has supposedly been privatised it's still under heavy state control. The government quango Ofwat decides how much water companies should charge for their product, which gives them no opportunity to compete through pricing on the open market in the way a normal company would; nor does it give them much incentive to become more efficient and plug all their leaks – they'll get paid just the same regardless of how crap they are, and it's not as though the customer has the ability to shop around and find another water company if his local one's no good.

As for us water users, what incentive do we have to take shorter showers or shallower baths – let alone heed Ken Livingstone's vile mantra, 'If it's yellow let it mellow/If it's brown flush it down' – when we get charged according to the rateable value of our houses rather than according to the amount of water we use?

Here's something quite useful to know, though. There's a PC government clause which expressly forbids water companies from cutting off their customers' water supply. This is why around 15 per cent of households never bother to pay their water bills and the rest of us have to stump up nearly one billion pounds extra as a result.

So what say we all stick two fingers up to this idiot system by refusing to pay our water bills until such time as our freedom of choice is restored? If we want to water our lawns till they're greener than a tree frog's arse we should be free, for a fee, to do so. If, on the other hand, we choose to let our cherished gardens wither and die so as to free up supplies for all those extra immigrants to wash in after they've done our plumbing, then we should damn well be rewarded for our sacrifice.

Welfare State

Bludger's charter. The Welfare State, we're always being told, is one of Britain's great post-war achievements, but the only people who actually believe this are Marxist historians, unreconstructedly Old Labour MPs, Polly Toynbee and Dave Cameron (*qv*). Everyone else just thinks it's a massive joke – or would do if it didn't involve so much of their money, stolen from them by the government and handed over in the name of social justice to:

1. Gangs of housing-queue-jumping, Vicky-Pollard-style career-single-mothers chain smoking fags so as to make their babies smaller.
2. 'Backache' victims who, now that they're permanently off work, need bags of state assistance if they're going to pay for their golf club membership, squash lessons, etc.
3. Reluctant slackers who'd actually quite like to earn a living but can't do so because the tax and benefits system makes it far more rewarding to stay on the dole, smoking weed and getting really good at *Countdown*.
4. Criminal gangs defrauding the system and spending their money on guns and crack.
5. Families like The Royle Family and that other, not-even-funny family on *Shameless*.
6. Abu Hamza; people who support the IRA; burglars; muggers; Labour voters; bad people generally who you really wouldn't want any of your money going to ever but over whom you have no veto because it's the dole office that decides, not you.
7. Almost everyone, in fact, who isn't you. It may well be that – thanks to Gordon Brown's ingenious plot to make more and more people beholden to the state so that no one votes Tory ever again – you are the only remaining person in the whole of Britain who doesn't receive some form of welfare benefit.

'Think the unthinkable . . .' Frank Field (the only decent Labour MP apart from Kate Hoey) was told in 1997, when Tony Blair put him in charge of much-needed welfare reform. What poor Frank didn't hear was the whispered bit at the end of the sentence, which went, '. . . And I'll sack you.'

White, Hideously

If, as its former director general Greg Dyke claimed, the BBC is 'hideously white', does that mean it's OK to call the Commission For Racial Equality, the congregations of gospel churches, the hip-hop record industry, US basketball teams and Brixton Road 'hideously black'?

Why? (see Aaronovitch, David)

Why Oh Why? (see Toynbee, Polly)

Why Oh Why Oh Why? (see Brown, Yasmin Alibhai)

Wife Beater, State Propaganda Adverts Accusing You of Being A (see also NSPCC)

So you've popped into the leisure centre for your morning swim and you're towelling yourself down in the changing room afterwards when something on the wall catches your eye. It's a poster of a nice, well-dressed, professional type with whom you're clearly supposed to identify. 'Relax, go ahead and read,' says the text underneath. 'No one can tell you're a wife beater.'

'Christ!' you think. 'They've found me out!' And you vow never ever to slap the missus about again because now you've read about wife beating in this Metropolitan Police poster campaign you suddenly realise it's wrong.

No. Not really. What you actually wonder is: since when did it become acceptable practice for the authorities to spend our money on offensive, intrusive ad campaigns directly accusing us of crimes we have neither committed nor are ever likely to commit?

And do they honestly think that the tiny minority of people they're aimed at are going to take the slightest bit of notice?

Apparently they do think that, because if you happened to be reading a lad's mag or listening to a credible music station in early 2006, you will have come across half-a-million quid's worth of similarly 'hard-hitting' government propaganda ads effectively accusing you of rape. Sexual intercourse should never take place, the campaign asserted, unless the female partner has first given her unambiguous consent. 'All men are rapists' wimmin used to say in the seventies, but in those days it was treated as a case of mildly amusing feminist hyperbole – not official government policy.

Wind Turbines

'How the hell did we let that happen?' we often ask ourselves when we look at the brutalist monstrosity tower blocks which we allowed to blight our towns in the sixties. In a few decades' time we're going to be asking exactly the same question about all the wind turbines ruining what's left of Britain's wilderness.

And a bit like the perpetrators of terrible sixties architecture now, no one's going to be able to come up with a satisfactory answer because, quite simply, there isn't one: wind turbines are a wrong and a bad idea in almost every way imaginable.

They don't work when there's no wind.

They don't work when it's too windy.

They produce so little power that even if you put one on every hilltop in Britain (see also Goldsmith, Zac) you'd still need to rely on nuclear to supply our energy needs.

They chew up flying wildlife.

They produce a subsonic hum which drives you mad if you're downwind of them.

They turn pristine landscapes into Teletubby-style horror shows.

They drive down property values.

They're visible for miles around, so that just when you're thinking you've got away from it all you're reminded of man's grim presence by the whirling white shapes on the horizon.

They're environmentally damaging: their bases alone require enough concrete to fill two Olympic-size swimming pools; then there's the access roads that have to be built through the unspoiled landscape to put them up in the first place.

They're monstrously expensive. Where gas, coal or nuclear power costs around 2p to 3p per kilowatt hour, power from land based wind turbines costs 5.4p and from sea-based ones 7.2p.

They make you feel a bit queasy, especially the three-bladed ones whose asymmetry is disturbing.

To supply the equivalent output of one nuclear power station you'd need a wind farm the size of Greater Manchester.

Apart from that though, they're a great idea.

X Factor Parents

Their daughters are fat. Their sons are ugly. The very brightest prospect that could possibly await their talentless, malodorous, tone-deaf offspring is a job on the Lidl checkout. Yet when Simon Cowell, not unreasonably, tells them these simple truths, they throw a massive wobbly.

Such is the terrible price we must pay for two generations' worth of Esther-Rantzen-esque anti-bullying policies, mixed-ability-classes and non-competitive sports days (*qv*). We're crapper than ever before – but none of us knows it.

Your Local Council

Your local council is brilliant: it tells you so on the lush brochure that drops unbidden through your letterbox each month and delights you with glossy photos of smiling, ethnically balanced toddler groups and uplifting stories about new recycling initiatives and breakdancing courses for pensioners and black history month events and Winterval and Kwaanza festivals (in the season formerly known as Christmas) all generously funded by lovely old you, the ratepayer.

Try getting any kind of personal benefit from the grand or more you fork out in council tax each year, however, and you're in for a long wait. Neighbours holding a noisy party? Oh dear, our Noise Hotline service only operates between 12 p.m. and 1 p.m. on Sundays in a leap year. Run out of compulsory orange bags for your recycling? Should have thought of that earlier: we need at least a fortnight's notice and in the meantime we reserve the right to fine you £1000 for incorrect rubbish disposal. Nearly killed, yet again, by one of the boy racers who has turned your once-sleepy avenue into a grand prix circuit? Unfortunately, our transport officer is on extended leave at present, but on his/her return s/he will spend thousands of your pounds on a lavish survey into local consumer attitudes towards all aspects of traffic management (which we will then bin and do what we were going to do anyway), after which s/he will send in a team of ten contractors who will spend three months building a single speed hump either so low it acts as an amusing incentive for racers to drive faster or so high it rips off the suspension of any car trying to negotiate it at speeds of greater than 2mph.

But that's not all. No longer content with being merely politically correct, corrupt, incompetent and profligate, our councils have recently taken it upon themselves to act as our environmental consciences as well. They have granted themselves the right to rummage through our dustbins, punish us for our choice of motor vehicle, and spend yet more of our money on hectoring leaflets lecturing us on how best we can reduce carbon emissions.

And who exactly are these people inflicting all this misery on us? Why, the sort of embittered lefties, crazed greens and loopy Lib Dems too talentless even to get jobs as traffic wardens, or social workers, let alone as MPs. Anyone who works for a council is, by definition, unfit to exert any form of control over another person's life. Yet that's what they do. Every single day of their lives. (Those rare days where they're not off sick playing billiards or on diversity awareness courses or on extended paid leave pending an investigation into the mysterious disappearance of last year's £10 million parks and leisure budget.)

Z

Zephaniah, Benjamin

Quite possibly Britain's greatest living poet. A titan, at the very least, to rank with Maya Angelou (*qv*).

Zoos

First to go, generally, are the elephants. Then the giraffes. Then the big cats. What the hell is happening to our zoos? Pretty soon, all that will be left for our children to see will be the goats in the petting enclosure, the leaf-carrying ants in the insect bit and the massive, great gift shop full of jigsaws, mugs and toys depicting all the fun, exciting creatures that used to be on display before zoos came over all worthy and animal rights and PC.

'Hey, kids, what say we pop down to the zoo and read a few interesting signs about conservation projects and breeding programmes? And if we're really lucky and we look very carefully in those new, special, animal-friendly display cages we might possibly glimpse part of a stick insect's forearm poking out from behind a tree. Then we can go home feeling really bad thanks to all the hectoring notices telling us how evil we are and how the devastation of the world's animal kingdoms is all our fault.'

And what is all this rubbish we have to put up with nowadays about man being The Most Dangerous Animal On The Planet? What about saltwater crocodiles, great white sharks, polar bears, lions, hippopotami, Cape buffalo, fierce snakes, Sydney funnel-web spiders, box jellyfish and all the other myriad creatures that could have most of us, easy, in a one-to-one unarmed combat situation?

The fact that any of these animals are still alive is largely due to the fact that we, as the planet's pre-eminent species, have generously allowed them to stay alive. If one or two of them need occasionally to be plucked from their natural habitat and shipped to a zoo, there to spend the rest of their days being gawped at by ice-cream-licking kids, well such is the price to be paid for not being king of the animals. Plus, it's not as though they don't get the odd perk. Pandas: a succession of tasty-looking breeding partners; seals: free ball-skills coaching; lions: drunks, nutters, daredevil teens and anyone else stupid enough to climb into their enclosure thinking, 'Well, they don't look very scary to me...'